Debt-Free at Forty-Three

Debt-Free at Forty-Three

How I Achieved Financial Freedom in My 40s Through Smart Saving, Spending, and Investing

Lorna Stuber

No part of this publication may be reproduced, distributed, or transmitted in any form or by any means—including photocopying, recording, or other electronic or mechanical methods—or by any information storage and retrieval system without the prior written permission of the author, except in the case of very brief quotations embodied in critical reviews and certain other non-commercial uses permitted by copyright law.

Cover design by MiblArt

Interior layout and formatting by Lorna Stuber

Copyright ©2021 by Lorna Stuber. All rights reserved.

Dedication

To my parents and grandparents, all of whom worked so hard their whole lives to provide for their kids and grandkids.

And especially to my mom, who taught me so much about being frugal while still encouraging me to seek and enjoy a fulfilling life.

With deepest gratitude to my skilled and
delightful editor, Andrea Idso.

Ancora imparo

—Michelangelo

Table of Contents

Introduction 1
   My Background 2
   Why I Wrote This Book 3

Chapter 1: Making a Mental Shift **9**
   My Story: My First Loan 12
   My Story: Be Happy with What You Have 17

Chapter 2: Finding the Right Bank **21**
   Determining What Each Bank Will Do for You 22
   Finding a Bank That Meets Your Needs 23
   Comparing Interest Rates 26
   Comparing Perks, Incentives, and Rewards 26
   My Story: Customer Loyalty Only Goes so Far .. 28

Chapter 3: Saving **33**
   Saving Versus Paying Down Debt 33
   Paying Yourself First 34

My Story: Filling Two Pots 37

Using Money Purposefully *38*
My Story: Fattening the Piggy Bank 41

Chapter 4: Attacking Debt **45**

Understanding Good Debt and Bad Debt *45*
My Story: Vehicles 46

Determining Which Debt to Pay off First *48*

Paying Less Interest *52*
My Story: Achieving Debt-Free Status for the First Time at Twenty-Five 57

Chapter 5: Finding the Right Credit Card **61**

Choosing One Credit Card: Use It but Don't Abuse It .. *61*

Using Credit Cards Wisely *65*
My Story: The Right Card for Me 66

Chapter 6: Opening Your Investment Accounts **71**

Getting Started with Investments *71*

Taking Advantage of the Registered Retirement Savings Plan (RRSP) *73*

Taking Advantage of the Home Buyers' Plan (HBP) *82*
My Story: Waiting for the Right Time to Buy a House 83

Chapter 7: TFSAs and RESPs **87**

Understanding TFSAs *87*

My Story: Using My TFSA Savings 90
Understanding RESPs 90
Managing Your Investments 91

Chapter 8: Making Your Money Make Money 95

My Story: Making My Money Make Money 97

Chapter 9: Real Estate 103

My Story: Operation Mortgage Annihilation! ... 112

Chapter 10: Determining Need Versus Want 115

Streamlining Your Life 115
My Story: I Only Buy What I Need 117

Determining Life's Essentials 118
My Story: Losing the Extra Weight! 120

Treating Yourself 125
My Story: Treating Myself! 126

Chapter 11 Saying No to the Upsell 129

Questioning the "Deal" 131
My Story: Recognizing That More Is Unnecessarily More 134

Chapter 12 Looking for Deals 143

Spending Wisely 143
My Story: Thrifty Shopping as Part of My Social Life 145

Bonus Story #1: Sometimes You Just Get Lucky! 146
Bonus Story #2: Accidental Savings 147

Taking Advantage of Sales.. 148
My Story: I Never Pay Full Price for Toilet Paper 152

Using Coupons and Member Discounts 154
My Story: Streamlining... 156

Chapter 13: Maximizing Your Tax Situation 159

Doing Your Taxes... 159

Claiming Tuition 161

Claiming RRSP Contributions...................................... 162

Claiming Deductions for Working from Home 162

Claiming Child Care and Other Child-Related Expenses 163

Claiming Health Expenses... 164

Claiming Charitable Donations.................................... 165

Claiming Professional Development (PD) Expenses.... 166
My Story: Donating What I Would Have Spent Anyway... 166

Chapter 14: Finding Money 169

Taking Advantage of Rewards Programs 171

Finding Travel Deals 172

purchase. By the time this book has been out for a year or so, our society may be back to where it was pre-2020. We may also see permanent changes in our habits and daily interactions as a result of the pandemic. It's hard to know where we are headed, but I aim to include timeless information that will serve you under most any circumstances.

Many of us have heard that in case of emergency, we should have the equivalent of at least three months' salary in easily accessible savings, but saving up this much money and keeping it aside for emergencies isn't easy. Costs keep rising, and salaries don't keep pace with inflation. A financial hit such as a sudden job loss or the ripple effect of an emergency like the pandemic can leave us in a position that seems impossible to conquer. And the older we get, the more discouraging and stressful a tight financial situation can seem as we start to look ahead to retirement.

IMPORTANT:

It's never too late to turn your finances around!

But there's good news! It's never too late to turn your finances around. While having a large amount of debt may seem overwhelming, taking small steps will reap great financial *and* psychological rewards.

This book is geared for those in their twenties, thirties, and even forties with little financial knowledge but high financial stress. It is written for people who wish to make financial freedom a priority by taking control of their finances, reducing debt, and making their money work hard for them. In this book, I share strategies and personal stories that will hopefully not just inspire you but also help you establish and maintain financial stability and strength. While you may not become a millionaire by age forty—or ever— you can improve your finances while still living an enjoyable, rewarding life and setting yourself up for financial stability in your later years.

But reaching financial stability takes commitment, sacrifice, and diligence. Implementing intentional strategies, while challenging and frustrating, has given me a fulfilling life—while reducing the amount of time and energy I spend worrying about whether I will be poor and starving when I'm eighty.

This book covers the main aspects of one's financial life. The content includes everything that is already part of your life, such as spending on essentials, choosing and using credit cards, and finding a bank. It also covers actions you may or may not already be taking, such as investing and buying a home. I have a few extreme examples of some lucky events that have happened to me along the way, such as winning a jackpot in Las Vegas. However, the principles and strategies in this manual are all within reach of the average middle-class person. The wild examples are illustrations to entertain you but also to help you start thinking about how you can apply different strategies to specific events and situations in your life.

I don't talk much about *Registered Education Savings Plans (RESPs)*. Likewise, I don't discuss budgeting for and spending on children in general since I don't have kids and I've never had to budget for children. But kids are expensive. If you have—or plan to have—children, you'll likely want to set aside money for their future education in an RESP. As they grow, you will also need money for their school fees, clothes, and hobbies. In this case, consider what I say in Chapter 2 about prioritizing and saving in general. I don't mean to diminish children to being just "expenses," but when it comes to spending money on them, many of the same general financial principles apply.

Money is a huge source of stress for a lot of people. Over the years, however, I have learned to break through that stress, change my mindset about money, and have fun with it. I've done this while making my money work as hard—or, ideally, harder—for me as I have worked for it.

I hope that you find this book informative and entertaining. Most importantly, I hope that my suggestions and stories will help you relieve at least a bit of your financial stress.

The COVID-19 crisis brought huge financial stress to many Canadians and people all over the world, with sudden job losses and fewer opportunities to make money while bills and expenses still loomed. In early April 2021, more than half of Canadians reported being $200 away from not being able to pay their monthly bills. The number of people in this situation had been creeping up over the years, and the pandemic pushed it over the 50% mark.[2]

I started writing this book before the pandemic was declared and have made some changes accordingly as a result of the shifts we've had to make. For example, one of my initial points was that although many people have moved away from using cash in the past decade or so, research proves that we spend less if we use cash. Therefore, I was all set to encourage you to use cash more. However, with the recent emphasis on limiting contact with other people and objects, I have been using the tap feature on my credit card in places where I used to use cash, even for a coffee

---

[2] MNP Ltd, "Over Half (53%) of Canadians within $200 of Not Being Able to Cover Their Bills and Debt Payments, Up 10 Points Since December Reaching a Five-Year High," Intrado Global Newswire, April 8, 2021, https://www.globenewswire.com/news-release/2021/04/08/2206577/0/en/Over-Half-53-of-Canadians-Within-200-of-Not-Being-Able-to-Cover-Their-Bills-and-Debt-Payments-Up-10-Points-Since-December-Reaching-a-Five-Year-High.html.

my savings account and be debt-free at twenty-five opened the door to greater financial stability and freedom over the next stage of my life.

As I said, I'm not a trained financial expert. But I'm financially savvy and my knowledge has served me well. As an ordinary middle-class person with no formal financial training, I'd like to think I'm walking, talking proof that achieving financial freedom well before your sixties is entirely doable. All it takes is a little knowledge and fair bit of effort and focus.

Why I Wrote This Book

We often hear media reports about the high levels of debt that Canadians are carrying. In 2017, the debt-to-income ratio in Canada reached an all time high of 179%, meaning Canadians collectively owed $1.79 for every $1 earned. In the first three months of 2020, we again neared that peak with the debt-to-income ratio reaching 175.4%.[1] Many people are living paycheque to paycheque, deeply in debt, and one misfortune away from financial hardship.

---

[1] Alexandra MacQueen, "Canada's Climbing Debt-to-Income Ratio: What You Need to Know," CIBC Pace It, December 2020, https://www.moneysense.ca/save/debt/canadas-climbing-debt-to-income-ratio-what-you-need-to-know/

tips in this book that will serve you well, plus a few ideas that may or may not.

My Background

I'm not a financial adviser, banker, or trained investment expert. I am a former teacher turned freelance editor, writer, and ghostwriter who has learned to squeeze money out of a seemingly dry sponge and save it in a metaphorical airtight bottle. With the help of sage advice from my mother and good professional advisers, a little hard work, and a lot of focus, I have gained the financial freedom that comes to most people only when they reach their sixties, if ever.

At forty-three years old, I became debt-free for the third time in my adult life. Barring any horrible, extreme, or unforeseen tragic events, I intend to maintain my debt-free status, including owning my own home, for the rest of my life.

In 1992, at age twenty-two, I landed in Japan to begin a two-year teaching stint. After two years, I had paid off my $14,000 student loan. I stayed for a third year, and in that time, I saved $25,000. Granted, $25,000 isn't enough to buy a private island or plan for early retirement. Indeed, it wasn't even enough for that back in the '90s! However, to have that amount of money in

Introduction

We all used to follow the rule, "Never talk about religion, politics, or money when you're sitting around the dinner table." Somewhere along the way, we've drifted away from following that rule. Every day on my Facebook feed I see a plethora of opinions on all sides about political and social issues that arise in the daily news. As a society, we may not have become as vocal over the years about money as we have about religion and politics, but I would be hard-pressed to tell you the name of a friend or family member with whom I have *never* had a conversation about money.

Opinions about money aren't necessarily as divisive as religious and political conversations. That said, this book *is* full of opinions. Take them or leave them, but until you try a strategy, you won't know if it will work for you or not. If you're drowning in debt and don't know where to begin, choose a handful of the ideas in this book, try them, and see how they work for you. Financial management is far from a one-size-fits-all mentality, but there are lots of tried-and-true

  My Story: Take the Deal 173

Generating More Income 175
  My Story: Selling Rocks 176

Generating Passive Income 177

Chapter 15: Using Unexpected Income 183

  My Story: Scholarships 184
  Bonus Story: Miss Oblivious Gambler 2012 186

Chapter 16: Taking Risks with Your Money 195

Conclusion 201

Glossary 207

About the Author 217

Index 219

Bibliography & Additional Reading 233

Chapter 1 Making a Mental Shift

Making and managing money are huge parts of every adult's daily life, so it only makes sense that money is sometimes a source of overwhelming stress. As children, we put our teeth under the pillow so that the Tooth Fairy rewards our toothless rite of passage with a quarter, a loonie, a toonie, or even a paper bill. At birthdays, we are excited if Grandpa and Grandma give us cold hard cash because we know we can take that physical object to a store or garage sale and trade it for something colourful, delicious, or fun.

    As we grow older, our mindsets transition. Once, we were excited about trading a little piece of metal or a colourful piece of paper for a candy or toy. As adults, we become stressed and perhaps even angry at the mere image of a dollar sign—and especially a bill that needs to be paid. When moving from childhood into adulthood, we have to start paying our own bills, buying our own clothes and groceries, and putting gas in the car that we may or may not have gotten as a sixteenth birthday gift. Or we may have to settle for public transit if we can't afford a vehicle. When we are teenagers, we can't wait to become adults. Yet when we reach adulthood, money stress becomes an ever-present part of our lives.

Why is even the thought of money so stressful? Is the answer as simple as, "Because I never have enough?" How much is enough? The cliché "Money can't buy happiness" is certainly true, but why is it that a lack of money causes so much stress? Probably because money is necessary. In order to satisfy our basic needs—food, clothing, shelter—we need money. And as time goes on, we need more and more of it. Life certainly isn't getting any cheaper.

But only having our basic needs met is not "living." We want more. Happiness in our society entails much more than having sufficient food, clothing, and shelter. To have a well-rounded life, many of us also want vehicles, vacations, kitchen gadgets, and a vibrant social life. The problem is that unless we are fortunate enough to be wealthy, we can't have everything all at once without going into debt— sometimes stifling debt. As with any aspect of life, balance is the key to finding fulfillment when it comes to making your money and then using it to enjoy your life.

The most stressful periods of my university life, when I was between eighteen and twenty-one and working on my teaching degree, weren't related to exams or essays or even the student teaching. The highest levels of stress I remember were during the last few days of most months while waiting for my next student loan installment to come into my bank account. My parents didn't have much money when I was growing up and so they couldn't put me through university. I had to rely almost entirely on my savings, money I earned from summer jobs, and, most heavily, student loans. Altogether, it was barely enough, and there were many times when I would be running on financial fumes at the end of the month. There were several times when I had no groceries—and no money to buy groceries—in the days leading up to those deposits, so all I had to eat were crackers, butter, and jam. Once in a short while, maybe once or twice per school year, I would have to call my parents and ask to borrow money from them to buy textbooks or groceries.

To this day, one of the hardest things I have ever had to do was call my parents, knowing how tight their money was, to ask for $100 on the promise I would pay them back in a few weeks. I felt like a failure and that somehow, I had let them down. I wasn't a failure, though. I wasn't skipping class to hang out in the bars and movie theatres, spending all my money on beer, movies, popcorn, and gummy bears. I was a young adult partaking of an expensive journey—higher education—and I was learning how to support myself on a meagre amount of money. My parents always came through after those phone calls, but I also always paid them back as soon as I got my student loan payments because I didn't want them to feel my financial pressure, and I didn't want them to think I was taking advantage of their help.

That guilt turned me into a responsible borrower, impacting the way I have approached loans to this day. I hate owing people money, even if "people" means the bank. The feeling of being financially indebted to someone has always felt smothering, and so since I was a teenager, I have tried to pay off my debts as quickly as possible. Not having a debt hanging over your head is so freeing.

My Story: My First Loan

I was thirteen when I took out my first loan. I was involved in the local 4-H club and our focus was horses, but we could also choose from some optional side projects. One that I chose was photography because I loved to take pictures. Shortly after getting into the photography option and learning a bit about the art, I realized my little Kodak Instamatic wasn't going to cut it. I decided I wanted a nice camera, and so I went shopping.

The jewellery store in my hometown also served as the camera shop. That's where we took our film to be developed (yes, I'm that old!). I looked at their options and settled on a nice Canon SLR. It cost around $200, which was more money than I had in my wallet or even bank account. (I had more money, but it was locked away and I couldn't access it! More on that later ….) And so I negotiated a deal with the shop owner to pay off the camera over several months. My payments were in installments of around $20 each, and I made a point of getting my butt into the store once a month to make my payments. I didn't have a job at the time. I was a farm kid and wasn't old enough to drive, but I struck a deal with my mom: I would take on milking the cow twice a day in exchange for getting the money from the sale of the cream.

And so that's how I paid off my camera. Lucy (our milk cow) and I met twice a day, she gave me her milk, and I took it into the house to separate it. My mom sold the cream to townspeople and gave me the money, which I then saved up and took to the store once a month to pay off my camera. I still remember how rewarding it was to see the shop worker pull out the index card with my tally on it, update it every time I made a payment, and then put it back into the drawer each month until ... finally, the balance reached zero. The camera was fully mine!

Having adopted this mentality of diligent debt repayment at a young age, I then transferred this thought process over to making money. As a young adult teaching in Japan (my first job out of university), I was sick of being stressed out about debt and worrying whether I would have enough money for groceries, and so I decided to take complete control over my situation.

I love a good challenge. I'm competitive by nature; I'm sure that competitiveness has helped me view debt as my opponent and take on the attitude that I want to "beat" it. And so I challenged myself to not only reduce and ultimately eliminate my debt, but also to start aggressively saving money. That way, I would reach the point sooner rather than later when I wouldn't have to worry about ever having enough money. If someone tells me I can't do something, I'm the type of person who will set out to emphatically prove that person wrong. I grew up in a family that had no money most of the time, and so I was determined to not continue to be in that position my entire life. Financial freedom was a challenge I took on at an early age.

When setting financial goals for myself, I knew that some of them were unrealistic goals I would likely not reach, but I also knew the great sense of satisfaction I would get if I did. I'm a goal- and checklist-driven person, and so setting goals or checkpoints for myself is extremely motivating. I get a bit of a rush when I check something off my list and then move on to the next checkpoint, aiming to tick that one off the list as soon as possible. If you are the same, start to think about your financial freedom goal list.

As a result of having this mindset over the years, I've developed a positive, take-charge attitude toward money. **I have come to see money management as a challenge, not a stress, and it's a challenge I have learned to overcome**. If you're serious about improving your financial situation, then you need to make some drastic, hard changes—and the first change is your mindset.

Feeling in control over my financial situation is a win for me and my competitive nature. I don't focus on having more money than another person or being better off than the neighbours. Rather, I focus on improving *my* situation over time, competing with myself, and being better off than I was last year or even last month. I also don't beat myself up if I don't quite reach my goal. I simply carry it over or adjust it for the next checkpoint and try, try again.

TIP:

Don't focus on having more money than someone else. Rather, focus on improving YOUR situation over time.

My competitive nature makes many of the strategies in this book work for me. If you don't have that competitive edge within you, you can still take these strategies and make at least some of them work for you. But that mentality of winning the battle of financial freedom is what keeps your eye on the prize. I encourage you to get obsessed with getting your finances under control if debt is causing you huge stress. Make it a priority, much like you would with daily exercise. Whether you're getting into better shape physically or financially, reaching your goals takes commitment and long-term hard work and focus. These two goals are, in fact, quite similar: You may not see huge changes in a few days, but by taking one step at a time, with constant and consistent effort, you can make significant change over the long term.

These days, I am in a good financial position, but I still make a game or competition out of saving and making money. That determination to pay off my camera loan when I was thirteen has carried over and served me well in saving thousands of dollars of interest and other unnecessary fees and expenses over the years. It's also helped me make thousands of dollars. For me, this challenge is fun and profitable.

My Story: Be Happy with What You Have

My three-year stint in Japan wasn't my first foray into living in another culture. When I was eighteen, after my first year of university, I spent six weeks living in a jungle camp in the interior of Peru doing volunteer work. That summer reinforced the world view that my upbringing had taught me, informed in part by my parents stretching their money to give my sister and me the opportunity for music and figure skating lessons. My loosely developed world view at that age was that people don't need much to be happy and live fulfilled lives.

During my summer in Peru, I saw so many families that had nothing, yet they were happy. By "nothing," I mean that compared to our lives in Canada and the U.S., they truly had nothing. I saw parents and children living together in shacks smaller than the chicken coop on my parents' farm, with probably only a couple of changes of clothing, growing their own food. In some situations, their family unit living under the same roof included grandparents, as well. And these people were happy. My encounters with them revealed generous, friendly, content people.

Since then, I've been to every continent except Antarctica (which is absolutely on my list), and I have seen how so many people live with so much less than we have in Canada and the U.S. European and Asian houses and yards are vastly smaller than ours, mainly because they don't have the available land that we have. What always resonates with me when I travel is that material possessions do not equate to happiness. In fact, the less people have, the happier and less stressed they seem to be.

I was in Germany for Christmas a few years ago and was fascinated by some of my observations of the season. Compared to the front yards overflowing with inflatable Frostys and Rudolphs that we see, the houses over there were decorated with plain white lights. Instead of mountains of presents under the tree, each person in the family I was visiting exchanged one or two meaningful gifts with each other. Germany at Christmastime reinforced for me that Christmas can certainly be beautiful and meaningful without the excess that many of us put into it here.

There is, indeed, a mindset here in Canada (and the U.S.) that "more is more." In fact, attempting to keep up with the Joneses often only increases stress because of the financial pressure we put on ourselves to obtain more. A big part of relieving that stress is deciding what you truly do need in order to be happy. I grew up with little, and therefore I always wanted

Chapter 1

more. But now that I have more, I actually want less because I've learned to find happiness in people and experiences rather than "things."

Chapter 2 Finding the Right Bank

Banks will compete for your business. Whenever you walk into a bank, you see promotions such as instant cash back for opening a new account and bonuses for transferring your mortgage from another institution. Some of these promotions are great. Take advantage of them if a bank offers you great perks for something you need, but don't lock yourself into a service you don't need just because it comes with an appealing perk. Instead of being lured by short-term rewards, find the right bank for you, and establish a long-term relationship with them. In particular, find a good investment adviser.

You may decide to change banks over time. I don't recommend changing often or even at all unless you have good reason. However, if a bank you chose at age eighteen isn't serving your needs any longer at forty, find one that does. You may not even choose to do all of your banking with the same institution, depending on which bank offers you what deal, and that's fine. I find it easier to streamline my finances and deal with only one bank right now, but there was a time I had accounts at three banks for different reasons, and that approach served me well. Give your business to whichever *bank* or *credit union* best serves your needs.

Determining What Each Bank Will Do for You

Whether you are beginning to set yourself up financially or wanting to switch from your long-term bank, determine your needs and find a bank that you feel comfortable with and trust. Your finances are one of the most significant parts of your life. Knowing that your finances are in good hands will help you grow your money and reduce your money stress.

Meeting with loan advisers and investment advisers at several banks is time well spent. You can decide which banks will offer you the best services and which advisers best meet your needs.

IMPORTANT:

Your finances are one of the most significant parts of your life. Knowing that your finances are in good hands will help you grow your money and reduce your money stress.

Finding a Bank That Meets Your Needs

Not all banks are the same. And just because your parents or friends bank at a certain institution, that doesn't mean it's the right bank for you. There are also credit unions, which have the same services as banks overall with some differences. For example, credit unions usually have lower fees and higher interest rates on some accounts than banks do. Credit unions are not-for-profit whereas banks strive to make a profit. For more detailed information, ratehub.ca's article "Banks vs. Credit Unions in Canada: What's the Difference?" outlines the differences clearly and succinctly.

When choosing a bank or credit union, consider your overall financial needs.

If you're getting your credit card through your bank, decide how many credit cards you need and why. I strongly suggest having only one—and finding a good one! However, there are special cases where more may be better. If you are self-employed, you may find it beneficial to have a business credit card as well as a personal one. If you spend a lot of time in the U.S., having one credit card in U.S. funds and one in Canadian funds may be useful.

Decide how much credit you need—emphasis on need, not want! Keep your limit on credit cards and personal lines of credit low so that you don't overspend and find yourself buried in debt—but do have enough credit so that you have ample available in case of emergencies. Remember, how much credit you have available and how often you use it will affect your credit score, as well. See the Glossary for more information about this.

Determine which of the following account types and services you need:

- savings or chequing account[3]
- Tax-Free Savings Account (TFSA)
- Registered Retirement Savings Plan (RRSP)

---

[3] You likely need one or the other but not both. Fewer people use personal cheques anymore, but look into the options that different banks offer. Some savings accounts will earn you a bit of interest. Maintaining a minimum balance in a chequing account may prevent you from having to pay some or all bank fees.

- Registered Education Savings Plan (RESP)
- other investments
- a mortgage
- a personal line of credit
- business accounts/credit cards

Examine what kinds of investments you currently have or want to have, and consider how much you know about investing: little to no knowledge, average knowledge, or a high level of knowledge. When you're deciding on a bank or credit union, meeting with a financial adviser should be part of the process. That adviser should be able to recognize your investment knowledge and risk tolerance, and then advise you accordingly. You should definitely feel comfortable when meeting with this person, as they are going to be responsible for guiding your financial future.

Find out which banks offer the accounts and services you are looking for. All banks will offer similar services, but choose what best fits your particular circumstances. Consider how well the staff at the bank recognizes and serves your needs, and look at how well the staff members at the bank personalize your experience versus simply trying to sell you on their services.

Comparing Interest Rates

I'll talk more specifically and in more detail about credit cards in the next chapter, but here I want to emphasize again that you should *compare the credit cards offered by different banks or companies*. And compare the interest that you can earn in different types of chequing or savings accounts. Savings accounts don't earn much these days, but if one bank offers you 0.1% interest on a savings account and another bank offers 0%, that's at least something to consider. That 0.1% may be worthwhile, or it may not, depending on other perks and options the bank offers you.

Get a credit card from a bank or company that is willing to negotiate and offer you lower rates. Paying 17% on your credit card balance compared to 25% saves you a lot of money in the long run if you can't pay off your credit card every month.

Comparing Perks, Incentives, and Rewards

Evaluate different credit cards and determine whether it's more beneficial for you to have a lower rate or perks such as rewards points. I know friends who have WestJet credit cards because they travel to a lot of places WestJet flies and their credit card gives them good benefits from WestJet, such as baggage fees waived, a companion ticket for $100, etc. Consider the perks that a particular credit card offers and choose one that fits your lifestyle. If you don't travel much, then the WestJet credit card won't serve you as well as a credit card that may earn you cash-back points, for example.

Here are a few pointers when considering the various rewards programs and perks attached to banks and credit cards:

- Ask yourself if the new client bonus for opening an account at a bank is worth committing to the bank for the long term.
- Compare service fees between banks.
- Ask the bank whether it will waive service fees if you have multiple accounts or maintain a certain minimum balance in your daily-use account.
- Look at what rewards or perks you get from various credit cards, and choose a card that gives you useful rewards for your particular lifestyle.
- Negotiate with your credit card company and your bank for better interest rates.

- Consider the long-term incentives for banking with a certain financial institution.

My Story: Customer Loyalty Only Goes so Far

When I was around eight years old, my mom opened a bank account for me and started teaching me how to use it. When I finished university and had to negotiate interest rates for my student loan, I went to my bank since they were the only bank I had ever dealt with. They did offer me what was a fair interest rate on my loan at the time, but perhaps I could have gotten a better rate elsewhere. I didn't realize at twenty-one years old that clients have a lot of options in banking and can shop around. I simply went with the bank I had been dealing with since my mom opened that first account for me.

As I started to build my investments in my late twenties, I saw that another bank had a better return on similar investments, and so I moved a bit of my money into that bank. For example, one mutual fund in my bank was earning me an average of 5.32% but the comparable mutual fund in a different bank was earning 5.62%. When I looked at the long-term averages, that mutual fund at the second bank consistently outperformed the first. Therefore, I switched that particular investment to the new bank.

Chapter 2

By my early forties, I had a mortgage with one bank, my main accounts with my original bank, and some investments with a third bank because of differences in interest rates and returns on investments. However, I had become increasingly dissatisfied with the local branch of my original bank. Whenever I wanted to see someone about investments, I requested the same adviser I had initially seen several years prior. But they kept scheduling me with someone new to their staff, and so I always had to start from the beginning, telling a different adviser at every appointment who I was and what my investment goals and strategies were. I had a good grasp on investing by then and grew increasingly frustrated that I was not able to deal with the same person and build a relationship with one adviser. I decided I was finished with this bank when two events happened.

First, I met with yet another new adviser about my investments. During the appointment, I felt she was not treating me as an individual by looking at my specific situation and needs. Instead, she was trying to sell me on the bank's services. I had gone to see her about moving some of my investments around, but before we even got into that topic, she tried to convince me to switch my mortgage to her bank. When I told her the terms and interest rate of my current mortgage, she quickly admitted she could not compete with them.

The original reason for my appointment was to sell off some of my high-performing investments and reinvest the profits into a different investment account. It quickly became obvious, however, that I knew more about those investments than she did, and she was not willing to do what I wanted her to do. I am a medium- to high-risk investor, and due to her lack of experience as an investment adviser, she felt I should be more conservative. I left the appointment feeling frustrated and annoyed at having to plead my case to someone who failed to recognize my needs.

A few weeks later, I requested another appointment at the bank to temporarily increase the limit on my line of credit. This time, ironically, I was scheduled to meet with the person I had continually been requesting to meet with regarding my investments. It was the first meeting I had had with her in two or three years, and she didn't remember me. She immediately refused my request for a credit limit increase, even though I told her the details of my entire financial situation. I explained that I would be able to pay off the balance of my line of credit in two to three months and just needed a small, temporary increase due to some upcoming house expenses. It was obvious she had her mind made up before I even explained the details of my situation. She wouldn't work to meet my individual needs and simply give me a small credit increase on my existing personal line of credit. Instead, she tried to convince me to apply for a *home equity line of credit (HELOC)*, which would have required me to borrow money against the equity in my house. I left that appointment frustrated again and promptly made an appointment with my other bank.

I had an established relationship with an excellent investment adviser at this second bank. I told her I was considering moving all of my finances over to her institution because of my frustration with the other bank. With my promise of paying off the line of credit as soon as inheritance money came my way, she immediately approved me for a new line of credit for the amount I was requesting. She also offered me a credit card that gave me far greater benefits than the one I had from the first bank. In the end, I moved all my finances to this bank, ending my relationship with the other one after more than three decades, because of personalized service and better value at the second bank. That lack of caring customer service drove me to look around—which, in the end, led to significantly better financial options and services for my needs. Having my investments at my new bank has also been much more profitable for me, as their investment funds perform better than the comparable funds at my previous bank. Win-win!

Chapter 3 Saving

Saving Versus Paying Down Debt

> **IMPORTANT:**
>
> *Saving needs to be a priority just as much as debt reduction does, even if you have a mountain of debt.*

You may feel like you want to put off saving money until you feel you can afford to and instead focus on paying down debt. If that's your approach, though, you may never get around to saving! You'll either always have debt or you'll always find something to spend your money on: vacations, new clothes, upgrades on technology or vehicles, and on it goes. Saving needs to be a priority just as much as debt reduction does, even if you have a mountain of debt. The best approach is to both save and pay down debt simultaneously so that you progress in both areas.

If you focus only on paying debt, you'll find that your debt is reduced but you don't have money set aside for emergencies or occasional treats such as vacations. You may additionally find that you've reached a certain age and don't have a good amount of retirement savings. Funding emergencies or vacations using credit will add to your debt load and may undo any progress you have made in paying down debt.

Conversely, if you focus too much on saving or don't put enough money toward debt reduction, in the long term you will pay a lot more interest on your debts than necessary.

Ideally, you will find a balance between reducing debt and saving money simultaneously.

Paying Yourself First

One of the best ways to save is to pay yourself first. Put 10% of all income into savings immediately. I know you're balking already. You've probably trained yourself to think you need to pay your bills first, and paying your bills is certainly important, but we'll get to that. Hear me out on paying yourself first.

On your paycheque, you will see *Canada Pension Plan (CPP)*, *Employment Insurance (EI)*, and income tax deductions have been taken before you've even received it. You may also have deductions for union dues, other dues, or other taxes. Because these deductions are taken off your income, this is money you never had in your pocket. If you approach saving 10% of your income in the same way, before long you won't notice this 10% reduction in the money that doesn't land in your bank account.

I've heard people say they don't have extra money each month to put aside. I said the same thing when I was in my twenties. If 10% is too high a number, start with a smaller amount. Start with 5%, $50 a month, or even $25. Start with *something*. You likely won't notice having $25 a month less each month. Set up a *Registered Retirement Savings Plan (RRSP)* account (which I'll talk about in depth later in Chapter 6) or even a savings account. Arrange to have that $25 or $50—or, ideally, 10% of your income—put into savings. After the first few months, you won't even miss that small chunk of change.

The easiest and best way to put 10% of your paycheque aside is to make the transfer or deposit automatic. Then you don't have to remember to move this 10%, and you aren't tempted to spend it. Arrange for one of the following:

- Have your employer take 10% to add to a company retirement plan.
- Set up automatic contributions to a savings or retirement plan at your bank, and have them deposited on or shortly after your payday. This is a great option if your employer doesn't have a retirement or pension plan.
- Open an RRSP account, and have your bank make automatic contributions to it each month shortly after you are paid.

As a teacher in a public school board, I had a pension plan, and contributions to it came off my paycheque before I even saw my paycheque. It was money I never had to begin with, and this is a great way to approach savings. Think of it as money you never even had. Better yet, don't even think about it. I never did. I always looked at my net income each month—the amount that went into my bank account. My pension contributions had been taken off before that amount was calculated, so for years I had money set aside every month that I didn't ever think about.

Having even a small chunk of money going into retirement savings every month and not even being conscious of that money means you will wake up one day, years down the line, with a tidy chunk of money set aside. Surprise! A nest egg! If you are paying into a pension plan at work, great! You're one of the lucky ones because these pension plans are less common than ever before.

If you don't have a retirement or pension plan through your employer, set up your own. If you can swing it, set one up even if you *do* have a plan through your employer! I did both, and believe me, it's nice to wake up when you're forty-five and realize you have two good-sized piles of loonies sitting and waiting for you to get old!

IMPORTANT:

Put 10% of your income into savings.

My Story: Filling Two Pots

I began taking this approach to savings early on in my career. I was twenty-five, had returned from Japan, and was teaching in Canada for the first time. I arranged for the bank to take 10% of my paycheque out of my account on the last day of each month and put it into my RRSP investments. The money wasn't taken out until my paycheque had been deposited, ensuring that my account was never overdrawn, but it was taken out soon enough after payday that I never noticed it. Like CPP, EI, and income tax deductions, it was money I never thought of as being mine and therefore never missed. Unlike those deductions, this money is still mine to manage today, and by putting it into an investment, I have that money working for me after I worked for it.

As my paycheque increased over the years, I adjusted the savings so that I was always putting in 10% of whatever my take-home pay was. I continued to do this even when I had a job in a public school system and was building my teacher's pension account. Now, I have two bundles of money I can use for retirement: my teacher's pension and my own RRSP accounts.

Using Money Purposefully

Another great way to save money is to make a habit of using cash instead of credit or debit cards. Research has shown that people who use cash rather than credit or debit cards are less likely to overspend.[4] If you can limit yourself to spending only what you have in your wallet, you are more conscious of how much money you are spending. You will also be less inclined to buy things you don't need. Financial

---

[4] Bill Hardekopf, "Do People Really Spend More with Credit Cards?" Forbes, July 16, 2018, https://www.forbes.com/sites/billhardekopf/2018/07/16/do-people-really-spend-more-with-credit-cards/#5c8b205d1c19.

experts commonly advise using cash as much as possible so that you can more easily track what you are spending and stay within your budget.

When the COVID-19 crisis hit, some stores stopped taking cash. Many asked patrons to consider paying with credit or debit cards to reduce the amount of physical contact with bills and coins being passed back and forth. Of course, this is worth considering, especially if you are a germaphobe to begin with, but if you do use plastic instead of paper or coins, keep track of what you spend. I'll talk about credit cards in depth later; using one has a lot of benefits if you manage it well, but you do have to manage it well!

If you use credit or debit, monitor how much you are spending by checking your bank balances regularly.

Following these steps will help you to manage your cash flow:

- Create a weekly spending limit and stick to it.
- Withdraw your weekly spending limit from your bank account and use this cash for your weekly purchases.
- If you are using credit or debit, keep track of how much you have spent in a week, and once you reach that limit,

stop. If you see yourself getting close to that limit well before week's end, cut back on your spending.

Are there expenses you can put off until the following week? Are there expenses you can eliminate completely?

For example, consider your coffee intake. Instead of buying an expensive latte every day, limit yourself to one or two a week and put the money you would have spent into a savings jar; the savings will add up quickly! Make your coffee at work, especially if it's free. Take advantage of the "buy nine, get one free" perks from places like McDonald's and 7-11. Or make it at home and take it with you in a go-cup.

Here's another built-in savings strategy when using cash:

- Spend paper money rather than coins, and at the end of each day or week, empty the coins from your wallet into a piggy bank or jar.
- Empty your coin jar every six months and deposit the coins into a savings account or exchange them for paper money and use the money for something fun. You'll be surprised at how quickly the coins add up, and when

you dive into it, it will feel like money you found!

Regularly putting away even a small amount of savings will benefit your financial health, but it will give you a psychological boost, too. You'll be practicing discipline, which can also be applied to other aspects of life, and you'll gain confidence in your ability to manage your money. As your savings grow, you'll gain optimism that there is a light at the end of your financial tunnel. You'll gain a sense of freedom as you take vacations or upgrade your vehicle without feeling guilt or stress over finances.[5]

My Story: Fattening the Piggy Bank

During the three years I lived in Japan, I used cash for almost everything because Japan was a cash-based society. There was no such thing as a chequing account, and people rarely used credit cards for purchases. My paycheque was handed to me each month in an envelope—a thick envelope stuffed with the equivalent of about $4,000 cash. I did have a credit card when I lived in Japan, but I only used it for large

---

[5] Kentin Waits, "7 Ways Psychologists Say Saving Boots Your Mental Health," WiseBread, December 15, 2014, https://www.wisebread.com/7-ways-psychologists-say-saving-boosts-your-mental-health.

purchases. I got into the habit of carrying and using cash, as all the locals did.

Japan's currency includes the following:

- paper money for ¥1,000 denominations (roughly Can$10) and higher
- coins for ¥500 (roughly Can$5) and less

I started spending only paper money and saving my coins. It was difficult to save the ¥500 coins because I would run out of money if I put them aside. I allowed myself to spend them when I needed to. But I saved all of my other change. When I sat down to roll my coins twice a year, I quickly discovered I was saving an average of $100 per month in coins. This money became part of my vacation fund.

I continued this habit of spending cash and saving coins for twenty years after coming back to Canada in 1995. When I sat down to roll my coins twice a year, I felt like I had found some extra money. It was money that I never thought about, and I continued to use it to fund my vacations (until my vacations became more elaborate and my finances became less strained).

Up to the declaration of the pandemic, I still mainly used cash unless it was a purchase so large that I didn't have enough cash in my wallet. Even now, I still never use my debit card for any purchases. I rely heavily on my credit card because of its rewards program (more about that later) and because of the impact of COVID-19.

Chapter 4 Attacking Debt

Understanding Good Debt and Bad Debt

You may have heard of good and bad debts. Student loans and *mortgages* are considered good debt because education and buying a home are good investments. Education is an investment in yourself, and the more skills you build, the better-paying job you can get as you go through life, so don't be afraid to spend on courses and training.

Bad debt is debt you have incurred from buying things that aren't necessary. Try to limit or even avoid bad debt as much as possible, and focus on using your credit for what you need to maintain a comfortable lifestyle.

Mortgages and vehicle loans are longer-term debts that most people expect to pay off over several years. Credit card debt should ideally be paid off every month. If you have a significant debt load on your credit cards or line of credit and can't pay these loans off in full every month, focus on paying them off. These are examples of bad debt, and they will cost you unnecessary interest the longer you take to pay them off. Interest accrued on vehicle loans and mortgages is part of almost everyone's life. Worry about those once you have the bad debt under control.

My Story: Vehicles

Vehicles are tricky. A lot of people recommend not buying brand-new cars because they depreciate so drastically. And they are right.

I do buy new vehicles, though, because I can afford them but also because I need mine to be reliable. Depending on where you live, you may need a vehicle. If you can get by without one, do. But I can't. I do a lot of highway driving, and so I need a reliable car. If you use your vehicle heavily (for work, for example), you may find it is better to have a new(er) vehicle you can trust. I'm not going to advise you to "invest in a vehicle" because they are not investments. They are 100% guaranteed to suck money out of you, but if you do need one, consider what you need out of your vehicle. Then buy the cheapest best option for you.

I didn't start buying new vehicles until I was well into my thirties because I couldn't afford the hefty monthly payments. When I did start buying new vehicles, I negotiated the car loan and made manageable monthly payments for five years until the vehicle was paid off. Then, I kept driving the same vehicle for another five years or more so I could enjoy not having a car payment. The benefit to having a new vehicle is that everything is under warranty and so you're probably covered if something goes wrong. The maintenance is minimal. For me, those monthly payments for a few years are worth the price, because I know I'm the only person who has ever driven the vehicle—and if anything goes wrong, it's under warranty. When my vehicles start getting older and needing more attention, I look at how much I'm spending on maintenance, such as brake work, new tires, other replacement parts, etc. Of course, a vehicle needs more attention as it gets older. Once I get to the point where I'd rather have a monthly car payment than be trotting my vehicle in for repairs—and then waiting a day or a week to get it back—I sell it and get a new one that I don't have to worry about. Time is money, too, and I'd rather use my time to make money or go for a beautiful hike in the Rockies than sit in an automotive garage for a few hours waiting for my vehicle to be fixed.

Determining Which Debt to Pay off First

What if you have multiple debts spread out in various places? Credit card debt, student loans, a car loan, maybe a balance on your *personal line of credit* because of that trip to Cancun last winter. All that debt is hanging over you, but you don't know where to start. It can be overwhelming and confusing.

Start by determining your priorities. What's most important to you—paying off the loan with the highest interest as soon as possible? Or paying off one loan and getting rid of it so you have fewer debts staring you in the face?

The *avalanche method* means you focus on paying off loans with the highest interest rates first while making minimum payments on all of your other loans. This approach will ultimately save you a great deal of money in interest charges.[6]

The *snowball method* takes a different approach. In the snowball method, you focus on paying off the smallest debt first. Once that debt is eliminated, you then focus on the next smallest and eliminate it, and so

---

[6] Ashley Eneriz, "Debt Avalanche vs. Debt Snowball: What's the Difference?" April 28, 2021, https://www.investopedia.com/articles/personal-finance/080716/debt-avalanche-vs-debt-snowball-which-best-you.asp.

on.[7] Some financial experts recommend the snowball method because of the psychological boost it gives you—that feeling of accomplishment and progress you get from having paid off a loan! How motivating to see the number of loans you have shrink!

If reducing your money stress overall is your priority and you are feeling smothered by the amount of debt you have, use the avalanche method. Focus on the debt for which you pay the highest interest, such as credit cards. Pay off that bad debt first. If you are anything like me, seeing a balance on your credit card probably stresses you out simply because you know that if you don't pay it off every month, you'll be paying hefty interest charges, usually at least 18% per year and often more than that.[8] Reducing this bad debt will hopefully reduce your stress level, too! The sooner you can eliminate this debt, the less interest you will ultimately pay. Ideally, you will get to the point where you pay off your credit card balance every month. That way, you avoid paying *any* interest on those high-interest cards. Paying off your high-interest loans first and keeping them paid off is a great way to save a lot of money in the long run.

---

[7] ibid.

[8] creditcardGenius Team, "How Credit Card Interest Works in Canada," creditcardGenius, updated May 3, 2021, https://creditcardgenius.ca/blog/how-credit-card-interest-works-in-canada.

Consider this: If you're paying $100 a month in interest on your credit card, that adds up to $2,400 over the course of two years, and that $2,400 could grant you a fun vacation or a nice new laptop. If you start to think of interest as money you are throwing away, which is exactly what it is, you will hopefully make moves to avoid paying as much interest as possible over your lifetime. Interest on a long-term loan such as a mortgage is unavoidable, but credit card interest is like throwing money in the garbage every month. It's money much better spent elsewhere.

TIP:

If you start to think of interest as money you are throwing away, you will hopefully make moves to avoid paying as much interest as possible over your lifetime.

If you are like most people who have a mortgage, yours probably gives you a lot of stress simply because the amount you owe is so high. Forget about it. Make your regular mortgage payments, and make the highest payment you can, but don't fret about your mortgage. As long as you are making your payments, it will get paid off eventually. There's no sense worrying about a huge mortgage that is going to be there for several years or even decades when you have other debt. Focus on the smaller, nastier debts that can be paid off more quickly and that cost you high amounts of interest.

If you're stressed out about the number of debts you have—and, in particular, if you have multiple credit cards—then take the snowball approach. It's common to have multiple loans: student loans, car payments, mortgages, credit card debt, and possibly a balance on a line of credit. Take a look at how many cards you have in your wallet. How many of those pieces of plastic come with a monthly bill? Out of those monthly bills, how many of them do you pay in full each month? You may even have multiple credit cards: your main Mastercard or Visa, plus credit cards for different retailers. If you are overwhelmed by the number of loans you have—and if having the fewest debts possible to pay is your priority—focus on your smallest debt, eliminating it as soon as possible. Once you have eliminated the smallest debt, then focus on the smallest remaining debt and repeat the process.

The main factor to remember here is that once you pay off one of those loans, don't rack it back up again! Keep your card paid off and focus on streamlining where your money is owed. If you have multiple credit cards, pay them off and close them one by one. Leave yourself with one credit card for all purchases. You'll have fewer bills to pay each month, and you can take advantage of one really good credit card rewards program.

Paying Less Interest

If you have multiple credit cards in your wallet and you can't pay off all of them every month, you may be paying a lot more interest than you realize. As mentioned in the previous section, paying off your credit card balance in full each month to avoid paying any interest is the ideal. But that may not be possible in your situation right now — and it may not be for a long time yet. If that's your situation, then consolidating your credit cards might benefit you twice over. Not only will it help you keep track of all your monthly payments by streamlining them, but consolidation could also save you a lot of interest. Here's how:

1. **Close all your credit card accounts except one — or close them all and open a new one.** If you open a new card, remember, you don't have to get a credit card through your main bank. Shop around between credit card companies and banks to get the best credit card suited to your needs. For example, most department store cards charge at least 22%

interest.[9] It's in your best interest to stay away from them, even if they offer you a great perk to sign up for the card. By contrast, a good credit card from your bank will cost you less in interest in the long run, and it can give you good perks, as well. A typical bank credit card will charge anywhere between 10–25% interest. Right now, the average Canadian credit card charges 20% interest annually.[10]

2. **Negotiate with your bank or credit card provider** to give you the best possible interest rate on your remaining card—the lowest rate you can get. The best approach is to simply ask! Anytime I have asked what my options were for a lower-rate credit card or for a card with better perks, I have been given several options. And if you need to get a bit more forceful, you could always say that you are considering going with a different bank or credit card company. The credit card provider may be willing to offer you a better rate if it means keeping you as a customer. Don't lie, but if you

---

[9] Ratehub.ca, "Store Credit Cards," accessed August 23, 2021 from https://www.ratehub.ca/credit-cards/store-credit-cards.

[10] creditcardGenius Team, "How Credit Card Interest Works in Canada," creditcardGenius, updated May 3, 2021, https://creditcardgenius.ca/blog/how-credit-card-interest-works-in-canada.

have a definite option for a better rate elsewhere, tell them and see if they are willing to beat it.

3. **If you need to buy something on credit, use your one card and pay it off every month.** If you can't pay it in full, then pay off as much as possible to reduce the amount of interest you ultimately pay. Remember, the ultimate goal is to be able to pay your credit cards off each month so that you don't have to pay any interest, so whenever you make any progress on lowering your credit card balance, don't rack it up again.

The other benefit to reducing your number of credit cards is the impact it has on your *credit rating* (credit score). Anytime you make a large purchase, such as a house, vehicle, etc., lenders will check your credit rating and decide how much they should lend to you—or even if they should—based on your *credit score*. You want your credit score to be as high as possible, showing that you are a good investment for the lender and that you are reliable, trustworthy, and able to pay the money back. The smaller your debt, both in terms of the total money you owe and the number of loans you have, the better your credit score will be. And conversely, the more debts and loans you have (including credit cards), the lower your credit score will be. This is because having access to a lot of credit from many sources indicates you need to borrow a great deal of money and may not be able to pay it back. Also, the higher your credit score, the better position you are in to negotiate lower lending rates.

If you can't pay off your credit card every month, use a lower interest line of credit for making payments or to pay off higher interest loans entirely. Again, consider that the interest rate on your credit card is likely at least 18% compared to the interest on a personal line of credit, which is likely in the ballpark of 4–10%.[11] That's a big difference, especially if you add up how much interest is accrued over the course of a few years! If you don't have a personal line of credit, open one. Pay off the balance of your credit card with your line of credit. Immediately, you will be paying an interest rate of probably at least 10% less. Then, aim to pay your credit card off every month so that you're never paying that 18-22% (or whatever the interest rate on your credit card is).

The danger here, though, is that you'll increase the balance on your line of credit over the long term. Make sure you don't! Just because you have access to credit doesn't mean you should use it. And if at all possible, don't use up all of your credit. Even if you

---

[11] Tamar Satov, "All You Need to Know About a Line of Credit," GreedyRates, updated August 7, 2021, https://www.greedyrates.ca/blog/what-is-a-line-of-credit.

have a $10,000 limit on your credit card, keep the balance to under $1,000 or $2,000 per month, or whatever you can fully pay off each month. As a former boss of mine use to say, "It's a limit, not a target."

Remember, the goal is to pay off debt entirely so that you eliminate not only the debt but also those interest payments. If you get to the point where you know you can pay off your credit card balance every month without borrowing to do so, then you can next focus on paying off that lower interest line of credit.

Here's another option you can explore. If you have multiple loans at the same financial institution—a student loan, a vehicle loan, credit card debt, etc.—ask your bank to consolidate them into one loan with a lower interest rate. Most banks will agree to do this for you. If yours doesn't, ask another bank about the option of moving your loans over to them to consolidate them. It may or may not be worth it, depending on any penalties you may have to pay, but ask! You might find some good options available to you. Having only one loan makes it easier to keep track of what payments you need to make each month. There's also a good chance you can negotiate a fair interest rate on this loan that's lower than you might already have on others. At the very least, it never hurts to ask!

Your goal, particularly for bad debt, should be to pay it off as quickly as possible. To achieve that goal, make the biggest loan repayments you can handle rather than the minimum monthly payment. If you only make the minimum payments, you aren't making any headway. Most of the time, your minimum payment is equal to the interest charges, meaning you likely won't make any progress on paying off the actual loan. You will only be paying interest—and you'll end up accruing interest on interest. Without putting yourself on the street or having to go for a week without food, hammer that loan with as much money as you can each month so that you reduce the principal and pay off the loan as quickly as possible. When you receive extra money, make extra payments against debt rather than buying something you don't need.

No pain, no gain, right? Well, putting as much money as you can toward debt reduction *is* painful. But the gain over time will be paying less interest than if you dragged out the loan, and you will free yourself of that debt sooner rather than later.

My Story: Achieving Debt-Free Status for the First Time at Twenty-Five

When I was living in Japan from age twenty-two to twenty-five, I had only one debt: my university student loan. Before I left Canada, I sold my car and gave up my apartment. In letting my apartment go, I got my damage deposit back! Extra money! I had to buy a new wardrobe for my job, and I took with me everything I figured I would need. As a fresh university graduate, I didn't have many valuable belongings, but I kept what I thought I would want upon my return and stored it in my parents' basement. I got rid of everything else.

My goal was to come back to Canada debt-free after two to five years in Japan. For the first two years, I put as much money as I could toward my loan while keeping enough money for living expenses and vacations throughout Asia. My minimum student loan payment was $200 per month, but I started by sending $500 each month and increased it as much as I could until I was sending $2,000 per month. Because I made debt payment my priority, I paid off my student loan within two years. In my third year, I continued to send $2,000 home each month, which enabled me to come home debt-free—and with $25,000 in my Canadian bank account.

Since returning to Canada in 1995, I have incurred several debts, including car loans and a mortgage. Before I bought my first house in my thirties, I was again debt-free. Then I paid off my house in nine years rather than twenty-five, which was my original mortgage term. I had secured what was called a 20/20 mortgage, meaning I was able to do both of the following each calendar year:

- increase my monthly payments by 20% of the original principal
- make a lump-sum payment of up to 20% of the original principal

From my first mortgage payment, I consistently paid 10–20% more than the minimum required payment. Making biweekly payments also resulted in paying less interest overall because the principal loan amount was reduced every two weeks rather than just once a month. Whenever I had extra money from gifts or from living below my monthly budget, I made additional lump-sum payments. Within a year, I had reduced my mortgage term from twenty-five to twenty-one years. By the time I received an inheritance seven years later, I had reduced my mortgage enough to pay off the balance—taking advantage of the option to pay up to 20% of the original principal.

You may not come into an inheritance, but you may get raises or bonuses at work, receive cash for holiday or birthday presents, or find other unexpected money coming your way from time to time. Any extra money you can put toward debt will greatly reduce the amount of interest you ultimately pay and shorten the term of your loan.

Chapter 5 Finding the Right Credit Card

You probably find yourself inundated at times with offers to sign up for credit cards, either by mail or when checking out at a department store. It can be difficult to resist signing up for credit cards when you are offered appealing bonuses. But having too many credit cards—and having the wrong types—can lead to overuse and unnecessary debt, not to mention that hit on your credit score.

Choosing One Credit Card: Use It but Don't Abuse It

Some people think that simply using their credit card is bad. However, using it often and paying it off each month show that you have good money management skills, and this will reflect well on your *credit rating*. You can demonstrate your effectiveness at managing money by making your payments on time, making more than the minimum payments, and not maxing out your card.

Aiming to have only one credit card that serves all your needs will require you to make fewer monthly payments. Therefore, you can streamline the number of loan payments you need to make each month as well as limit the amount of debt you incur. You can also maximize your ability to rack up points or perks if you are using one card instead of spreading your spending around to multiple cards.

Not all credit cards are created equally. If you travel and want a credit card that is accepted easily worldwide, Visa or Mastercard would be your best options.

Even within those two choices, you have a lot of options. Every bank and a lot of businesses now offer their own version of these two credit cards. A WestJet Visa or a WestJet Mastercard are popular options for people who like to travel because of the benefits that come with these cards, such as waived baggage fees and cheap companion tickets.

Because every credit card comes with multiple options, start by establishing which cards you qualify for. For example, some require you to have a minimum

Chapter 5

annual salary, so if you don't meet that minimum, then the choice is made for you. Cross those off the list. List and review the cards you do qualify for, and compare the different perks and options they offer.

Decide what kind of rewards you want to earn:

- **Travel bonuses**: points you can cash in for flight tickets, access to airport lounges, waived baggage fees, free or reduced-priced tickets for travel companions, or hotel discounts
- **Cash-back bonuses**: points that you can redeem for cash

Most rewards cards charge an annual fee. Check what it is and determine whether the perks you earn are worth paying this fee.

WARNING:

Most credit cards with great rewards programs charge an annual fee. Make sure this fee is worth paying.

Determine whether you will be able to pay off the balance each month:

- If yes, then the interest rate doesn't matter. Look for other perks.
- If no, then shop around for a low-interest-rate credit card.

Determine how much credit you need:

- Consider how much credit you need to access.
- Ask yourself: If your credit card limit were high, would you be prone to spending more just because you could? If that is the case, keep the limit lower to force yourself to control your spending.

Make your one credit card a Visa or Mastercard rather than a store-specific card:

- Bank-issued credit cards typically have *much* lower interest rates than store cards.
- Department store credit cards can only be used at the store where they are issued unless they are a Mastercard or Visa connected to a department store.
- Mastercard and Visa are widely accepted around the world, but American Express is not. Even within Canada, many businesses do not accept

American Express because they have to pay higher fees to American Express than to Visa or Mastercard.

If you do get a store credit card, get it, keep it long enough to take advantage of the perk you get, pay it off, and cancel it. Remember, the more credit cards you have, the bigger the impact on your credit score. Also, the more you spread out your rewards programs, the longer it takes you to earn enough points in each program that add up to worthwhile rewards.

Using Credit Cards Wisely

- Use your credit card for purchases, but be sure to remain within your budget. If you have a great rewards card, then don't hesitate to use your card for everything; you'll accumulate more points faster the more you use your card. Just make sure you can manage the payments.

- Pay the entire balance of your credit card every month to avoid interest charges.

    NOTE: If you can't pay the full balance one month, use a lower interest loan, such as a line of credit, to pay it off. Don't make this a habit, though. Pay the credit card off with the line of credit, and then limit your spending so that you can pay the credit card off in full each month while paying off the line of credit.

My Story: The Right Card for Me

I got my first credit card when I was a second-year university student. The credit card companies were lurking around, ready to pounce on young, unsuspecting, deer-in-headlights students, and I was a prime candidate. I entered university thinking that debt of any kind was horrible and that if I wasn't careful, it would chew me up and spit me into a pit of fire. I wanted to avoid debt as much as possible. My student loan was the only exception because I needed to borrow that money in order to obtain my education. (Remembers student loans are good debts; education is an investment in yourself and your career!)

When I dared touch the credit card application, which was offering university students prime rates on a Visa card with a $500 limit, I felt as though I was on the verge of committing a serious crime. However, I stepped forward, applied for that Visa card, got it, and then was afraid to use it for fear I would rack up $500 of debt I would never be able to pay back. I did end up using the card once in a while; times were tough, and there were days when I absolutely needed groceries before my next student loan installment dropped into my bank account.

Chapter 5

I rarely maxed out my credit card, but when I did, I was sure to pay it off as quickly as possible. Being terrified of debt, and having only a $500 limit on that card, allowed me to start using a credit card without putting myself at risk of getting in over my head. It was a great learning experience, managing that $500 pit for three years. I gave up the credit card when I moved to Japan since managing it from there in the 1990s, before the days of the Internet, was too cumbersome. (Yes, I'm old enough to remember those days!)

When I was back in Canada, though, in my twenties and thirties and struggling to stay within a budget, I kept the limit on my credit card to $1,000 so that I would not overspend. At times, the bank raised my limit without asking me and when I noticed this had happened, I called them to set the limit back to $1,000. As I got older and was more capable of managing my money, I began to request small increases as needed for larger purchases.

I now have one credit card, and I use it often. At present, with our post-COVID-19 fears of touching surfaces, I don't handle cash. I pay for everything using the tap feature with my credit card to reduce the number of surfaces I touch. The card I have suits me well because I travel a lot. I earn points that I can use for travel: plane tickets, hotels, car rentals, or vacation packages. My credit card also gives me free access, four times a year, to a number of airport lounges. When I am travelling, I can enjoy waiting there instead of at the gate. If you have a credit card with a great rewards program, and you know you can pay your credit card off every month, use it! Use it a lot! Just make sure you do pay it off every month in order to avoid nasty interest charges.

I used to use my credit card for any purchases more than around $30; since the onset of the pandemic, I use it for everything. The points add up quickly, and my rewards program gives me bonus points for purchases such as groceries. I double-dip with my most common purchases: I buy my gas and groceries at the same business because all my purchases count toward my points program with that grocery chain *plus* I earn points on my credit card. Also, when booking flights, I get the credit card points *plus* the points from the airline.

I use my credit card heavily, but I also pay it off every month. My credit card rewards program has served me well. In the first five years after getting this credit card, these are the flights I took by cashing in the points I earned:

- Calgary – Honolulu – Calgary (Business class!)
- Calgary – Whitehorse – Calgary

- Calgary – Las Vegas – Calgary
- Calgary – Los Angeles – Calgary
- Calgary – Sydney (Australia) – Alice Springs – Sydney – Calgary
- Calgary – Bonaire (Caribbean) – Calgary
- Calgary – Panama City to … oops! To nowhere! That vacation got cancelled because of COVID-19. The good news is, because the cancellation was due to travel restrictions, the points were returned to my account, leaving me with a hefty chunk of points in my account to use for the next vacation.

All these within five years! Many would have been expensive flights, but with the money I would have spent anyway, I got them for free!

Chapter 6 Opening Your Investment Accounts

This is the "boring-est" chapter! (Yes, I like to make up my own words!) I put it in the middle because it's kind of like a Wednesday—once you're over it, you have something to look forward to. But, also, in the natural flow of your financial life, it's better if you think about investments sooner rather than later. Be sure to consider what I've said in the previous chapters before you make any bold moves about investments, though.

Getting Started with Investments

When you're in your twenties and even thirties, retirement seems so far away. But this is exactly the phase of your life when you need to start thinking about saving for retirement because of two words:

compound earnings. I'll get to that more specifically, but first things first.

There have been rumours for years that the CPP isn't going to exist for future generations even though we all pay into it. Who knows if this is true or not; we will all find out when we get there. Regardless of the CPP's status, fewer companies and organizations have retirement or pension plans for their employees anymore. Civil servant jobs include a guaranteed pension. But unless you are a teacher, police officer, MLA, MP, or any other government worker, chances are your employer isn't helping you much or at all when it comes to putting money aside for your retirement. And we are living longer now than previous generations were, so you will need money for probably at least a good twenty years or more after you leave the workforce.

I'm a big fan of putting as much into an RRSP as you can — as soon as you can. Why? Because you get money back on your income tax, and who doesn't want money coming back to them every year? But also, an RRSP investment is *tax-sheltered,* meaning you don't pay any income tax on any of it until you withdraw from it. Every bank you walk into has posters on the wall or signs on the desks showing you examples of how much $50 invested today could earn *compound interest* over the years. That $50 bill you save today will earn you a lot over thirty to forty years.

Chapter 6

Over the past thirty years, the Canadian government has introduced options like RRSPs, RESPs, TFSAs, and so on. What the heck is all of this? And which do you need? Well, those answers depend on your specific circumstances. I would argue that everyone should have an RRSP first and foremost and then a TFSA at some point, as well. Because I don't have children, nieces, or nephews, I've never opened an RESP; you may open one, five, or none.

Let's look at each of these investment types.

Taking Advantage of the Registered Retirement Savings Plan (RRSP)

As I mentioned, fewer and fewer employers offer pension plans to their employees anymore. If you are a civil servant or an employee in a large corporation, you will likely have some sort of pension plan that you contribute to with each paycheque. If you have a pension plan through your job, celebrate!

Even if you have a workplace pension plan, but especially if you don't, RRSPs are a great, great idea.

Let's go on a bit of a tangent for a minute: Remember when I said you should be putting 10% of your income into savings? What I didn't talk about much at that point was that financial experts recommend having the equivalent of at least three to six months' salary set aside in case of emergencies.[12] That chunk of money could be in a plain old boring savings account, or it could be in an RRSP. The only problem with having it in an RRSP is that you will need to pay tax on it if you take it out. So if you are a bit skittish and anticipate that you might need to tap into that emergency fund, keep it in an easily accessible savings account or a money market fund that you can quickly withdraw from.

TIP:

Have the equivalent of at least three to six months' salary set aside in case of emergencies.

OK, tangent over.

As you are building up that emergency fund, and especially after you have that money set aside, put as much as you can into your RRSPs. Start with

---

[12] Andrew Goldman, "Emergency Funds: What, Why, & How Much," Wealthsimple, updated March 15, 2021, https://www.wealthsimple.com/en-ca/learn/emergency-funds.

contributing even $50 a month—more, if you can swing it.

The type of RRSP account you open will depend on your age and your risk-tolerance level. The younger you are, the more risk you can tolerate. If you've been on this earth long enough, you will remember the economic crashes of early 2020 and 2008, the latter being when the housing marking bubble burst. In 2001, when the World Trade Towers were attacked, the markets—and, in particular, the travel industry—were temporarily hit hard. Markets swing; there will always be ups and downs, and if anyone could accurately predict those fluctuations, we could all easily make our millions on the stock market. No one knows exactly when the dips and spikes will occur, but we know they will occur at times.

Because you can expect market swings over the course of twenty to forty years, when you are investing for the long term, you can count on times when your investments drop and other times when they spike. If you can tolerate volatility, medium- to high-risk investments begun at a younger age can reap good rewards over time. If you have a low tolerance level and you know you will not be able to sleep at night seeing that you've lost $10,000 in a day because of wild market fluctuations, stick with lower to medium risk. Your investment adviser can advise you well in this regard. **I cannot stress enough: Find a good**

investment adviser and work closely with them. I am not going to give you specific investment advice. I'm not qualified to do so.

Once you get closer to retirement, you will want your money in lower-risk investments to protect it from those unpredictable swings. As you get into your sixties, you certainly don't want to lose large chunks of your hard-earned money when you don't have twenty or more years ahead of you to recoup your losses. Get yourself a great investment adviser through your bank or an investment company. (I know I already said this; I will keep saying it because **you do need professional guidance in this area**.) To find someone who will guide you, you'll need to do the following:

- shop around
- refrain from committing to any one fund or organization until you find someone you trust
- get recommendations of investment advisers from friends and family
- choose someone you feel comfortable dealing with

The best thing about RRSPs is that up until you are seventy-one, they are tax-sheltered. This means you could put $1,000 into an RRSP at the age of twenty, watch it grow for the next fifty-one years, and not pay tax on the growth until you take it out. Once you turn seventy-one, you have to start withdrawing from your RRSP. You can withdraw before age seventy-one, but you are only required to once you reach that age. So you potentially have roughly fifty years of your work life for this pod of money to grow before you ever have to pay tax on it.

Not only that, but here is my favourite part: Any money you put into your RRSP is a tax credit for roughly 30% of your investment. This means that for every $1,000 per tax year you contribute to your RRSP, you will get approximately $300 back, either as a tax refund or as a credit toward what you owe on your taxes. If you have to pay a fair amount in income tax every year, putting as much as you can into your RRSP will help you get a "discount" on your income tax payments.

When you are young, you likely don't earn as much as you will later, and therefore you likely don't have as much to put into your RRSP. But consider this example scenario: You have income tax taken out of your paycheque each month, and, as a result, you don't owe any tax when you file your return. Putting $1,000 into your RRSP for that tax year will get you in the ballpark of a $300 credit on your income tax return, which you would receive as a refund. You can then use that $300 to pay off credit card debt, make an extra payment on your mortgage, or (here's the fun part) put toward your RRSP. The latter will earn you a refund of around $100 on next year's tax return. Suddenly, that $1,000 that you contributed has earned you $400 in *addition* to what the investment itself may have earned in interest.

Here's an idea if you really want to get adventurous: Consider getting an RRSP Line of Credit from your bank.

WHOA! "Aren't you anti-debt, Lorna?" Yes, indeed I am, but keep in mind there is good debt and there is bad debt. Your mortgage is good debt because over time, you will pay it off and your home will be yours. All yours. Credit card debt is bad debt unless you pay off your credit card or line of credit every month without accruing any interest. An RRSP Line of Credit is *great* debt if all the following specific circumstances apply:

- You have enough room in your RRSPs that you can contribute in a particular tax year. (Your last income tax assessment from the Canada Revenue Agency [CRA] will indicate how much room you have for RRSP contributions.)

- It is February and the RRSP deadline is looming. (The contribution deadline is March 1st every year.)
- You don't currently have enough money to contribute (more) to your RRSP.
- You know you will be getting a tax refund, or you at least won't have a balance owing after completing your tax return.
- You can get your taxes filed by early- to mid-April and therefore get your tax refund back well before the end of April.

Borrowing the right amount of money to put into your RRSP before the contribution deadline (March 1st) will get you enough of a tax refund to pay off the loan. Borrowing this contribution right before the deadline will mean you'll pay little to no interest if you a) file your tax return as soon as possible and b) pay the loan off as soon as you receive your tax refund.

Let's look at an example:

It's February 2022, and you will soon be preparing your 2021 tax refund. You have a good sense of your tax situation for 2021—enough income tax was deducted from your paycheques, and so you will not owe any additional income tax. In fact, it looks like you will be getting a $1,000 refund after you file your tax return. Your RRSP contribution limit is $10,000, meaning you can put up to $10,000 into your RRSP without penalty, but you have no extra money to make an RRSP contribution before the March 1st deadline. You know, however, that you are going to get a tax refund of around $1,000. Aw! Bummer! Wouldn't it be nice to have that $1,000 first so you can put it into your RRSP now?

Wait! You can! You could use an RRSP Line of Credit to borrow the money for your contribution. If you put $1,000 into your RRSP before the deadline, you would get an additional $300 (ballpark) tax back in addition to the $1,000 you're already getting back—so why not borrow the $1,300? Then, when you receive your tax refund, you can pay off the $1,300 loan right away! If you time it right, you can do this without paying any interest—or at most, one month's worth, which would be negligible—and you then have an additional $1,300 in your RRSP account growing for you now rather than waiting to contribute.

This strategy works if you make sure you manage the timing. Know by mid- to late February what your income tax situation for the prior year looks like, and plan to file your taxes as soon as you have all of the required information. Your tax return will be in your bank account within a couple of weeks of filing your taxes electronically, and so, as mentioned, you can pay off that line of credit before you are charged much (or even any) interest. You're borrowing against the future, but it's the near future, and you're generating more income with that tax return without it costing you anything.

Your RRSP contribution limit per year is based on your income, and the limit carries over from year to year. So if you can't max out your contributions, and most people can't, you can contribute as much as possible each year. You will be penalized if you contribute more than your limit allows, so just review your tax assessment each year to see what your current RRSP contribution limit is. Contributing as much as you can will earn you tax-sheltered income for as long as possible.

TIP:

Borrowing the right amount of money to put into your RRSP before the contribution deadline (March 1st) will get you enough of a tax refund to pay the loan off.

Taking Advantage of the Home Buyers' Plan (HBP)

But what if you want to buy your first home and you are saving money for the down payment? Won't putting money into your RRSP make it take that much longer to get the down payment together?

No! Quite the contrary! In Canada, the *Home Buyers' Plan (HBP)* allows first-time homebuyers to borrow money from themselves for a down payment! You can borrow up to $35,000 from your RRSP to put toward the down payment of a home. This is the only time you can withdraw from your RRSP without paying tax on the withdrawal. The catch? You have to pay that withdrawal back within fifteen years. But that's not a bad deal. And as a bonus, you don't have to start repayments until the second year after taking the money out. Review the Canada Revenue Agency's HBP web page for more detail on this, as the amounts and terms may change from year to year.

What's great about the HBP is that your RRSP money can grow within a tax-sheltered investment until you need it for a down payment on your first home. Even better, when you use that money, you don't have to pay tax on what it may have earned! You just have to pay yourself back within fifteen years. Even better, you and your spouse can *each* make this

$35,000 withdrawal, and so together, you have a pretty significant down payment.

Worst-case scenario, if you can't pay yourself back for the HBP in time, then you do have to pay income tax, but let's hope you don't get to that point. Fifteen years to pay off a $35,000 loan from yourself? That's less than $2,400 per year or $200 per month. You can do it! And the HBP may allow you to get into owning your own home earlier than you would have otherwise.

As a bonus, if you have at least 20% of the purchase price of your first house as a down payment, you will not be required to pay fees from the *Canada Mortgage and Housing Corporation (CMHC)*. I will talk more about CMHC fees when I get into real estate investment in the next chapter, but for now, just know that it's another fee to avoid paying if possible.

My Story: Waiting for the Right Time to Buy a House

When I returned from Japan with that $25,000 in my savings account, I was coming back to my home country ready to start the next phase of my life, whatever that might look like. While living in Japan, I had decided that because I loved teaching English as a Second (or third, fourth, etc.) Language and had always been deeply interested in other cultures, teaching ESL was the career path I wanted to continue down. So I came back to Canada intending to go back to school to get a formal ESL and linguistics credential and then look for a job. I had myself convinced that to get a great ESL teaching job, I would have to be open to moving to Toronto or Vancouver, since those were more likely to have a variety of ESL schools where I could work. In Calgary in 1995, that $25,000 would have given me a great start on owning my own home! As much as I wanted to put it toward a down payment for a house or condo, I decided to hold off, thinking I would be in Calgary for a year and then end up moving east or west.

It's a good thing I made the decision I did, because with paying tuition, buying a car, and getting myself set up in an apartment with furniture and household appliances, I quickly blew through a large chunk of my savings. The good news is that I was offered a great job teaching at a new ESL school in Calgary halfway through my one-year ESL diploma, and so I quickly started making a decent, steady income. Still, it wasn't the right time for me to buy a house or condo, and so I started putting some money into my RRSP instead and using some money to travel, as well.

My decision to hold off on buying a house ended up being a good one even though it meant another ten years or so went by before I took that step. Yes, in those ten years, I could have paid off ten years' worth of a mortgage, but I didn't want to be *house poor*—a situation when a homeowner is stretched to the limit financially because their mortgage and home upkeep suck them dry financially. This can happen when people get into home ownership too early, before they have enough financial stability to cover all of those homeowner expenses, such as landscaping, building a fence or deck, or developing a basement or garage. If the house is older, it might need paint or a flurry of new things, like flooring, a furnace, a water heater, or windows. Sometimes the benefit of buying a house to start building equity so that you are no longer paying rent is diminished by all of the added expenses you have by being a homeowner rather than a renter. When you're renting, the landlord pays for the new furnace. When you own your own home, that's all on you!

     By the time I bought my first house, I was well into my thirties and had enough saved for a down payment—enough that I didn't have to pay CMHC fees. At that time, the withdrawal limit for the HBP was $20,000 compared to the $35,000 that it is today. I took $20,000 out of my RRSPs and paid it back within five years so that my RRSPs were again earning income for me while I was starting to build equity in my house.

     In my twenties, I wasn't yet ready to be a homeowner. I would have been too stretched financially, and so it was best for me to keep paying rent until I could afford home ownership.

Chapter 7 TFSAs and RESPs

Understanding TFSAs

A *Tax-Free Savings Account (TFSA)* is exactly that: a savings account where you can park money and let it grow tax-free. It's similar to an RRSP with two main differences:

1. You don't get a tax refund based on your contributions to a TFSA.

2. You can withdraw from the TFSA without paying tax on the money you take out. There are restrictions, though. For example, you can withdraw as much as you want one year, but you cannot replace it—i.e., deposit that amount back in—until the following year. The amount you withdraw will be added to your allowable contribution the

following year, so if you withdraw one year, for the rest of that year you can only deposit whatever contribution room you had before the withdrawal.

Many of the same investment funds that you can invest in for your RRSP, such as mutual funds and exchange-traded funds (ETFs), are available for TFSAs, as well. Check with your bank or investment company to see what funds are available for each type of investment.

Your TFSA contributions are limited each year, just as your RRSP contributions are. The limit has been $5,500 per person per year for most of its existence, but the federal government has increased and decreased that from time to time. As with your RRSP, the limit carries over every year, so if you have never put money into a TFSA, you have a lot of room for contributions right now! Also, like with RRSPs, I recommend putting as much as possible in your TFSA since these are tax-sheltered investments. You never have to pay income tax on what these investments earn.

TIP:

Put as much as possible into your TFSA since these are tax-sheltered investments.

Another benefit of TFSAs is that you can withdraw from them each year. Therefore, a TFSA is a great place to save money for a large purchase such as a vehicle, a vacation, home renovations, etc. You can take out as much as you like every year. Of course, you can't withdraw more than what you already have in the account! And you don't ever have to pay yourself back as you do with the HBP. A TFSA is a great investment if you know you will have big expenses in the near future. It's also a great parking lot for that emergency fund that should hopefully equal or exceed the equivalent of three to six months' salary.

As with your RRSP contributions, setting up monthly contributions to your TFSA will make it easier to contribute regularly and ensure you are saving money! You likely don't have $5,500 at one time to contribute to your TFSA. If you contribute up to $450 per month, though, you will be within your limit for the year. If you don't have $450 each month, contribute as much as you can up to that amount so that your money earns tax-sheltered income for you. The contribution limit for each year kicks in on January 1st each year, so if Santa has been good to you, you may have $5,500 to contribute right away. Whatever dollar amount you can put into your TFSA, contribute as much as you can up to the $5,500 limit throughout the year as soon as you can.

Check out the Government of Canada's complete guide to TFSAs.

My Story: Using My TFSA Savings

With inheritance money I received several years ago, I was able to contribute my full TFSA limit. Now, each year, I aim to contribute as much as possible up to the yearly allowable amount. When it came time to buy a new vehicle a couple of years ago, I took the money out of my TFSA and paid cash for my nice new ride! No tax payable on the TFSA, no problem. Having a brand-new vehicle felt great, but so did not making vehicle payments and knowing that I had saved a bundle of money, tax-free, to give myself this gift. The following year, I was then allowed to contribute back to my TFSA as much as I had withdrawn for my vehicle purchase.

Understanding RESPs

A Registered Education Savings Plan (RESP) is similar to an RRSP and a TFSA in that it allows you to contribute to an investment and earn tax-sheltered income on that investment. The purpose of an RESP is to set money aside for a child's post-secondary education while the child is growing up. As with RRSPs and TFSAs, there are limits to how much you can contribute and regulations regarding withdrawal of the money.

As I mentioned, I don't have kids and have not set up an RESP for anyone else's kids. Any adult who wishes to can set up an RESP, whether it's for their child, grandchild, or a friend's child. If you have kids or are planning to have kids, setting up an RESP is a great way to make sure there is money waiting for them when they start their post-secondary education. If they don't go on to further education, the money comes back to you, and you have to pay tax on the interest earned at that time. If the recipient does go on to post-secondary education, then grant money is also available to match a small portion of what is in their RESP. Starting with a small contribution when a child is young allows the money to grow over the years and ultimately takes a bit of the pressure off what with ever-increasing tuition costs.

For more information on RESPs, check out the Government of Canada's RESP web page and talk to your investment adviser.

Managing Your Investments

We've already looked at how you can maximize a tax refund by getting as much money into your RRSPs as possible—and as soon as possible. We've also looked at how you can put some money away each year, have it earn income for you, and never pay tax on what you earn by putting money into a TFSA. And I've talked a bit about RESPs—hopefully enough to convince you that if you have or will be having kids, an RESP is a great way to put money away for their education.

FULL DISCLAIMER: I am not an investment adviser, and so I want to re-emphasize that you really do need to find an investment adviser at your bank or at an investment company to give you personalized guidance.

Do some legwork. Find someone who can advise you over the years as to where the markets are going, what products are new and promising, and the specific types of investments that suit your individual needs and risk-tolerance level. Banks are safe starting points if you are a little nervous and new to all of this. You will make money on your investments in a bank over the long term. The intent of this book is not to serve as investment advice, because you have so many options, and you really need to work with someone who will advise you based on *your* situation. Look for someone you trust who will serve you well. Every bank has investment advisers you can consult.

Once you've found that person, meet with them once or twice a year to review your investments. I will talk a bit more in the next chapter about specific actions to take to make your money grow. But for now, think of meeting with your investment person to attend to your money just as you would meet with a professional to attend to your teeth, eyes, blood pressure, or vehicle. Your money needs to serve you as long as your body does—and much longer than your current vehicle does. Give it the same attention and upkeep that you would give your body and vehicle.

REMINDER:

Your money needs to serve you as long as your body does. Give it the same attention and upkeep that you would give your body.

Chapter 8 Making Your Money Make Money

I'm guessing you've heard the expression "buy low, sell high" in relation to the stock market? Well, your RRSP investments are not necessarily in individual stocks on the New York Stock Exchange (NYSE). But they probably are in mutual funds, dividend funds, bonds, growth funds, or some type of managed funds that are attached to the market but not as risky as buying individual stocks.

I'm not going to get into the differences between dividends, bonds, growth funds, etc., at this point because, again, I'm not an investment adviser. I know what I like and why, but you need to talk to your adviser to learn about what's best for you. If you have a good financial adviser, start by trusting them to guide you. If they are good at their job, they should ask you a lot of questions about yourself to get a sense of your investment goals, your risk tolerance, and your degree of investment knowledge. All of these factors will determine what types of investment funds you choose to put your money into. You don't need to be an expert on the different types of investments; you just need to have a good sense of what you want your money to do and what you're willing to risk to reach your goals. Over time, you will learn more about each type of investment.

Markets fluctuate, so be aware of whether you can tolerate watching your investments plummet at times. They will take a dive now and then, but markets always rebound, even though it may take a while—in some cases, a few years.

Regardless of whether your money is in a TFSA, an RRSP, or a chequing or savings account, you don't want it just sitting there doing nothing. At the very least, you don't want to be paying any more in fees than you have to, but everything you do comes with a cost.

NOTE:

You don't need to be an expert on investments. You just need to have a good

Chapter 8

sense of what you want your money to do and what you're willing to risk to reach your goals.

My Story: Making My Money Make Money

When I first opened my RRSP account and told a co-worker about it, his advice to me was to put the money in and forget about it for thirty years. At the time, I was teaching ESL at a private language school, and he was our Business English teacher. I didn't know much about investing, so I figured his advice was good. However, because I'm a naturally inquisitive person and a control freak who likes to know what's going on, I promptly threw his advice to the side. I started watching my investments—if not every day, at least a few times a week. I wanted to see what was happening, and when they started growing, I got even more curious.

Something in my farm girl upbringing kicked in. Every year when I was a kid, my parents planted a ridiculous number of potato plants, and every year, we dug up enough potatoes to last our family the winter and then some. In the spring, we then took what was left of the previous year's potato harvest and planted it. We used the "profits" of our potato crop to generate more potatoes. I took this approach with my money starting in my childhood.

When I was eight years old, my grandpa started giving me $100 each Christmas. I used it to buy a calf from my dad in the spring and then sold the calf in the fall, usually for around $600 to $1,000, depending on the cattle market prices. As per my mother's advice, I then put my profit into a Canada Savings Bond. That was back in the '70s and '80s when savings bonds were yielding an average of 10% interest. I continued this pattern each year with the money I got for Christmas until I left high school and moved away for university.

By the time I hit high school, I had earned a nice little bucket of money from my childhood investment strategy. These savings enabled me to buy my first vehicle and plan for attending university. My savings bonds were locked in for a certain time frame, so I couldn't cash them in for several years; most of them were timed to "unlock" around the time I finished high school. My mom had ensured that my investment, and its accrued interest, would be there for me when I got older and needed it.

This was before the days of RESPs. Today, the same logic and approach applies to parents setting up RESPs for their kids. Put money in every year, lock it away, and let it grow until the kid is ready for post-secondary!

Chapter 8

I carried that approach over into my adult investments. For example, if I invest $20,000 and see it grow to $24,000, I skim off my profits ($4,000) and reinvest them in something else. I still have my $20,000, which continues to grow, but I have another $4,000 growing elsewhere. Over the years, I have gotten into the habit of seeing my investment adviser on average twice a year to review my investments. Depending on what the markets are doing, sometimes I call her up and say, "I need to meet you to move money around!" If the markets are up significantly, even if I had only been in to see her three months prior, I take the opportunity to skim my profits and reinvest them. "What goes up must come down," and when markets jump, there is a chance they will drop again, so I reinvest the profits when I can. Then, when things drop, I haven't "lost" anything—in fact, I have gained, because by skimming profits and buying something new, I have a new investment that can earn me money when the markets go up again.

This is called *compound earnings*. Compound earnings include not just the interest you earned off of an investment but also the interest you earn off of *that* interest! Think of my parents' potato harvest: They started by planting X number of potatoes in the spring, they harvested X plus Y number of potatoes in the fall, ate Y potatoes during the winter, and then planted X again in the spring. The initial investment is always there. You earn on that and then take your earnings to earn more. This theory also applies to that RRSP example I gave earlier: When you put $1,000 into your RRSP, you get a tax credit of around $300. If you put that $300 into your RRSP, you get another $100, so you're earning off of your earnings. This is one of the best ways to make money.

Remember that credit card that earns me free plane tickets now and then? There are a couple of catches:

- To qualify, my annual income had to be above a certain level.
- There is also a $150 annual fee for having the credit card. However …

My wonderful guru at the bank told me how I can get around paying this $150 annual fee, and in fact, how I can exempt myself from *any* bank fees. And so for the past few years, I have paid zero bank fees. I have no limit on withdrawals, deposits, e-transfers, etc.! And no charges for any of that! The catch? I have to maintain a balance of $6,000 in my chequing account. That's it. If I meet that one requirement, I don't pay any banking fees, including that $150 annual fee for my magical, plane-ticket-generating credit card.

At first, the idea of keeping my balance that high was a bit daunting, but as I did with all of my other investments, I put that $6,000 in there and adjusted my mentality. Instead of seeing that as money I have and can use, I have convinced myself that instead of zero, my bottom balance on my chequing account needs to be $6,000. I think of it this way: If my bank balance goes below $6,000, then I will be overdrawn. The thought of having to start paying those fees again prevents me from going below a $6,000 balance, but **I also have $6,000 easily accessible in case I have an emergency.** By adopting that mentality, that $6,000 has become "forgotten" money—it's money I have and can use in case of emergency, but it's also money I don't think about. In my mind, it's not there. Physically, it *is* there, and it easily saves me $200 or more a year in bank and credit card fees.

Hmm, what shall I do with that extra $200?? That's a nice day trip on my next vacation. Swimming with the dolphins, perhaps?

Chapter 9 Real Estate

For most of us, our biggest monthly expense is our rent or mortgage payment. This won't go away until we pay off a mortgage, and for most of us, that will happen when we are in our later years. For some people, it may never happen. The thought of being in my sixties or older and still making payments for rent or a mortgage when I'm looking at retirement—and, therefore, having a much smaller income each month—makes me cringe. For me, the idea of being rent- or mortgage-free is hugely liberating; it eliminates my biggest monthly expense. If you are content to have that expense the rest of your life, then maybe long-term renting is for you. I just knew I wanted to eliminate that colossal monthly payment as soon as possible to take financial pressure off myself in my fifties and beyond.

I can't even begin to do the math, but I can tell you that paying a mortgage off in fifteen or even twenty years instead of twenty-five will save you a lot of money in interest payments in the long run. I mentioned this already: Consider making mortgage payments biweekly (every other week) instead of monthly. There are two advantages to doing this.

The first is that you make payments more frequently, and so the first payment each month reduces your interest charges. The reduction in interest charges starts immediately with the next payment. For example, you'll pay interest on a $300,000 loan for four weeks at a time instead of two weeks' compounds over time. So paying every two weeks will ultimately reduce the interest you pay over the entire term of the mortgage.

The other advantage is this: Consider how many months there are in a year. Twelve. That's easy math—even I can do the math in this paragraph. If you are making monthly mortgage payments, you make twelve payments in a year. Cool. However, think about splitting your monthly mortgage payment in half and paying that amount every two weeks. You end up making twenty-six payments over the course of a year, which works out to thirteen "months." You're essentially making the equivalent of thirteen monthly payments in a year instead of twelve, which also will save you a lot of interest over the long term.

Let's look at an example:

- Monthly mortgage payment: $800 per month = $9,600 per year
- Biweekly payment: $400 every two weeks X 26 weeks = $10,400 per year

That's an additional $800 payment per year. If you can do that right from the beginning of your mortgage, you will pay off the principal much more quickly. You will also accrue a lot less interest over the twenty years, or however long your mortgage lasts.

TIP:

Make your mortgage payments as high as you can handle.

The other way you can shorten your mortgage term and ultimately pay less interest is to make your mortgage payments as high as you can handle. If your paycheque is $4,000 per month, I don't suggest making your mortgage payment to be $3,000 per month. You need money to live, of course, and you also should be putting money into savings. You do need those treats now and then, too, so sit down with a piece of paper, calculator, and pen to calculate your monthly budget.

You will need to make a minimum mortgage payment, so make that payment and increase it as much as you can afford to. Most mortgage brokers and bank lenders suggest you stick to paying no more than 25–30% of your take-home pay on your mortgage payments so that you don't overextend yourself. However, if you have no other debt, you can surely afford to make higher mortgage payments without running short of cash.

Here's a starting point for you. It's a hypothetical example, so plunk your own numbers in:

- Combined monthly household net income: $6,000
- Savings (minimum 10% of net income!): $600
- Minimum mortgage payment: $1,000
- Groceries and toiletries: $1,000
- Gas and vehicle payments: $1,000
- Clothing: $200
- Entertainment (movies, eating out): $200
- Utilities: $800
- Other (school fees, kids' activities, pet expenses): $1,000
- **Total expenses: $5,800**

This is just a rough example, but in this case, your monthly expenses, including putting 10% of your net income into savings, add up to $5,800. This means you have an extra $200 each month. How about adding even $100 to your mortgage payments, still leaving yourself that final $100 cushion? An additional $100 per month into your mortgage is another $1,200 every year. That will make a difference quickly! You might not see much progress at first because of the interest on a high principal, but after a few years your mortgage will noticeably start to drop, and that progress is really exciting. Also, on those months when you don't spend money on clothes, for example, you can take any extra money and either add it to your savings or make additional mortgage payments. A drop in the bucket, over time, will help fill the bucket.

NOTE:

An additional $100 per month into your mortgage is another $1,200 every year!

I mentioned the CMHC in an earlier chapter. CMHC sets out the rules and regulations regarding home buying in Canada. For starters, CMHC requires you to make a minimum down payment that is 5% of the home's purchase price. I recommend that you have at least 10% of the purchase price to not stretch yourself too thin financially. Ideally, it would be great to have 20% or more for the down payment. First-time homebuyers who don't have a minimum of 20% of the purchase price of a house are required to have CMHC insurance. You'll pay this insurance's fees, so if you default on your mortgage, then the bank (or whoever lent you the money for the purchase) is protected. The payment to CMHC will be anywhere between 2.8%–4% of your mortgage.[13]

Remember, as a first-time homebuyer, if you have a good chunk of cash in your RRSP, you can borrow from yourself by taking money out of it through the HBP. And if you have at least 20% of your down payment, you don't need to worry about CMHC fees. That 2.8%–4% also adds up over time.

The other topic I want to address here is investing in real estate that is not your home but an investment property. It's become popular over the past few decades for people to buy rental properties—or, when they move to a new home, to keep their previous home and rent it out. There are advantages and disadvantages to taking these actions.

---

[13] Ratehub.ca, "Mortgage Default Insurance (CMHC Insurance), updated January 11, 2021, https://www.ratehub.ca/cmhc-mortgage-insurance.

Chapter 9

First of all, consider whether you can financially swing owning two or more properties. Remember, as a landlord, you are not guaranteed that someone will be paying you rent every month. You may have a month or two, or more, when your rental property sits empty, and during that time, you will be responsible for paying two mortgages. Sure, the idea of having a renter pay your mortgage for you sounds great, but what if you don't have a renter for a couple of months or even a year? The market is quite unpredictable at times. Also, depending on where you live, the rental market may be a struggle. In Alberta, when the oil sector has taken a huge downturn and jobs in the oil patch disappear, people tend to move out of province looking for work. So consider whether you can swing two mortgage payments for an extended period of time if vacancy rates suddenly increase because of unpredictable economic downturns.

In light of this possibility, would you take that chance? Or would you be more comfortable not having that rental property and instead investing in a mutual fund or another type of investment? There are plenty of fund options, depending on your risk level and your level of financial security. Consider what you are willing to risk and what the potential gains could be. Having a great renter who pays on time, takes good care of your property, and lives there for several years (ultimately paying a good chunk of your mortgage for you) is great, but that may not be what happens. You can hire a property management company, but then you have an additional expense.

Do you want to hire that property management company? Or do you want to the be the one who gets the 2 a.m. phone calls in February when the renter calls to tell you the furnace has quit? It then becomes your responsibility to spend time and money to fix that furnace ... or deal with a flooded basement, or replace the roof when a hailstorm shatters it. Also, if you have a renter who defaults on the rent, you will ultimately have to evict them. You could possibly also need to pay for repairs if they have damaged your property ... and all this after they haven't paid you rent for three months, for example.

Some people love that responsibly and want to be landlords; others don't. I toyed with the idea of having a rental property but ultimately decided I didn't want to be responsible for taking care of more than just my own home. For me, there were better investment options.

Lots of people have also started flipping properties. You've probably watched or at least seen promos for TV shows about this process. *Flipping* is simple in theory: You buy a cheap property, fix it up, and then quickly sell it for a profit. It is also a bit of a gamble because you are relying on making money on the property shortly after buying it, which may be out of your control. Flipping requires a few elements:

- **Being good at doing home renovations** or having readily available, reliable contractors who are good at their work.

- **Being on top of the housing market**, looking for cheap properties, and timing your purchases and sales of properties so that you actually make money.

- **Plenty of time.** Flipping is like another job.

- **A lot of money upfront!** Obviously, you have to buy the property to begin with, and you can certainly borrow to buy it, but you need to have access to that that type of cash flow. You also need to front the money for the repairs and upgrades. If you have a good stash of money available, you can do this. Once you have flipped a few properties, you can churn that money around, using the profits from one house to buy the next one, but again, it takes a lot of capital upfront.

Flipping is an awful lot of work. If home renos are your passion and you have a high risk tolerance, this might be a good strategy for you.

NOTE: As soon as you sell a property other than your residence, you have to pay tax on the capital gains. *Capital gains* are defined as the difference between what you paid for any investment and what you sold it for. So investing in real estate isn't as simple as getting profit; there are tax implications, too. This is where a good accountant comes in. If your nine-to-five job pays you a decent wage and your income places you in a higher tax bracket, then flipping or selling investment property might result in a heftier income tax bill than you want to pay.

My Story: Operation Mortgage Annihilation!

When I bought my first house, I set myself up for biweekly payments *and* I immediately started with payments that were a few hundred dollars more than the minimum payment I was required to make. My mortgage was called a *20/20 mortgage*, meaning I could increase my payments by 20% of the initial principal every year, *plus* make a lump payment each year of up to 20% of the initial principal. From the onset, I took advantage of both of these options as often as I could by putting as much against my mortgage as I could afford and was allowed to.

Chapter 9

By making biweekly payments, higher-than-required payments, and annual lump-sum payments, I was able to take a $250,000 mortgage down to $75,000 in just eight years, and when I received $72,000 in inheritance money, I paid off the remaining $75,000 in one more year. I was able to make a $50,000 lump-sum payment, which was 20% of my principal, plus make $1,200 biweekly payments. I had initially signed up for a twenty-five-year mortgage, and after just *one year* of diligently making higher-than-required biweekly payments and an extra lump-sum payment, I had reduced my term to twenty-one years. In the end, I paid off my mortgage in nine years. Imagine how much I saved myself in interest charges over the long term. THOUSANDS and thousands of dollars. Plus, I no longer have my largest monthly expense: a mortgage payment. The money I would be using for monthly mortgage payments gets me great vacations and goes into savings, where it earns me even more money in other investments.

A few years after paying off my house, I sold it and moved to a different town. Knowing that I didn't have to deal with mortgage negotiations—and that I was the full owner of my home—also made the paperwork a lot easier! No financing, no worry about *liens*, etc. No having to finance the purchase of a new home. And I also didn't have to worry about the purchase of my new, beautiful home falling through if I couldn't get my finances organized.

Chapter 10 Determining Need Versus Want

Streamlining Your Life

The more you have, the more you want! Does this sound familiar?

There has been a big push in the last few years for all of us to reorganize and declutter. Some of us have adopted this approach and tried to apply it to our lives. But not everyone has.

Life really is less stressful when we have fewer tasks on our calendar, fewer demands on our time, and less clutter in our houses. I don't imagine there are too many of us who actually enjoy tripping over the clutter on the living room floor.

We all likely have a lot of material possessions that we simply don't need. Getting rid of them declutters your physical space but also your mind, at least for me. Likewise, we all have a lot of digital and virtual clutter. Take a look at how many apps you have on your phone. How many of them do you actually use? I probably use fewer than half of mine, yet for some reason, I have a hard time uninstalling the ones I've never even opened.

There are loads of books that talk about how to declutter your closet, your cupboards, and your basement. Let's talk about decluttering your expenses.

Take stock of your monthly expenses. How many subscriptions do you pay for? Amazon Prime, Netflix, Spotify, more, more, more. These monthly charges add up over time. The monthly fee of $9.95 to Spotify works out to basically $120 per year. That may not seem like much, but how many other subscriptions do you pay for, and what do they cost you per year? I have Spotify, and I also have a SiriusXM subscription. Do I really need both?

- Can you downsize and consolidate some of these expenses so that you can still have the entertainment and services you want without paying any more than absolutely necessary?
- Do you feel that you get what you pay for?

If the answer to the latter question is no, cancel those subscriptions. Be discerning. There are probably a lot of things you pay for that you can live without and not even notice over time.

My Story: I Only Buy What I Need

I'm self-employed and work at home, so my utilities, to a certain extent, count as business expenses. But even though I get a bit of a tax credit for some of these expenses, I still don't spend more than I have to on utilities. I don't have Netflix. (I feel like I'm the only person in the 21st century who doesn't, although I know that's not true.) I find enough on regular cable TV to keep me entertained, and if I do want to watch a movie, which is rare, I simply rent it on demand. It's not worth it for me to have the extra subscription.

I do have SiriusXM and Spotify because I listen to music pretty much constantly during my waking hours. When I'm taking a road trip, Sirius allows me to listen to my favourite channels from anywhere in Canada or the U.S., and I also have it playing on my computer when I'm home working. Spotify allows me to pull up any song, album, or podcast anytime I want to listen to something specific.

I try to get as much mileage out of my cellphone, vehicle, etc., as I can. I don't buy the latest cellphone version when it's out; I upgrade to a new one when my phone starts acting wonky and when I see a good deal an upgrade.

Same with my vehicle. I do buy new vehicles, but I drive them for years until they start acting up and costing me money for repairs.

Determining Life's Essentials

Go through your closet. How many shirts, pants, dresses, suits, and shoes have you not worn in a long time—or **never** worn?

Go through your kitchen cupboards—same question. How much stuff do you have that you never use? How much of this stuff can you get rid of and never miss?

Better yet, **don't buy the stuff in the first place!** Sure, if you can sell something you no longer need and get a little money out of it, that's great. A few years ago, I took two garbage bags of clothes to a consignment store that still had the price tags on them! Selling them for a few dollars was better than donating them or throwing them away, but spending $60 on something I never wore even once and then selling it for $5 is obviously a waste of money. Get rid of stuff, but even better, check your buying habits, and work toward not buying stuff that you don't need.

TIP:

Get rid of stuff you don't use. Better yet, don't buy stuff you don't need!

Obviously, we all need food. But how much food do you end up throwing away? I know I'm not alone in regularly ditching stuff from the crisper in the fridge because I forgot about it or just never got around to cooking it before it started getting hairy. (It really should be named "the rotter" instead of the crisper, because that's where veggies go to rot!) I'm particularly bad about cilantro. I buy a lot of cilantro because I love it, and I always have good intentions of making salsa, but before I "get around to it," the cilantro has wilted. Change your habits. Either use the stuff before it goes bad or buy less of it so that you aren't throwing food into the composter. Food = money because, after all, you did pay for the food! Quit throwing five-dollar bills into the compost bin.

Do you own a vehicle? Do you *need* to own a vehicle? Some of us do, but if you live in a city with a decent transportation system, maybe you can get by using that instead of having your own car. The annual price of a transit pass is miniscule compared to the cost of gas, oil changes, car payments, maintenance costs, and … speeding tickets!? Insurance in particular is expensive, not to mention the price of the vehicle to begin with. Yes, relying on public transportation might be inconvenient, but is the convenience of having your own vehicle worth the price of it? Only you can answer that because it depends on your financial situation and your need to freely get around. If you only use your vehicle for driving to and from work and the grocery store, maybe getting a transit pass to save a ton of money is a change worth making. Tweaking your lifestyle to use public transport will be an adjustment at first, but it may ultimately be worth it.

My Story: Losing the Extra Weight!

About six years ago I set out to become healthier physically and mentally. I lost eighty pounds over the course of a year. Naturally, I had to buy a lot of new clothes at various steps along the way, and in doing so, I cleaned out my closet and got rid of the clothes that were too big for me. I found a great consignment store, and so I made a little money off of my discards. In the end, I got rid of **ten garbage bags full of clothes, many of which I had barely or never worn.**

Freeing up that space in my closet was mentally freeing, as well. My closet had been jam-packed because I had such a huge amount of clothes. After I downsized my body and my closet, I could actually look through my clothes without having to forcefully push others to the side! There was space in my closet! I swore I would never let my closet get so packed full again.

Losing weight is great, but so is losing clutter.

In the past ten years, I've been responsible for downsizing several households. With a number of deaths in the family, I have helped multiple family members downsize their homes, and I've dealt with handling estates. It's true that whenever someone moves, purging comes naturally. I've helped with five moves of different aging family members in the past ten years, as well as my own move within the past year.

Every time I helped with one of these moves, a significant amount of stuff went into the garbage or into boxes to donate to thrift stores. One of the best feelings I've had in the past couple of years came from standing in front of a bin at the landfill, throwing, with all my strength, glass or metal into the bin and hearing the CRASH! It was cleansing!

Throughout these moves, I was amazed at how much stuff people accumulate over the years that ends up just sitting and collecting dust. I looked at my grandfather, my father, and even myself and asked the question, "How much of this stuff does someone actually need in order to be happy and fulfilled?" The answer came in the form of the garbage bags full of stuff that I got rid of.

Even when I moved *into* my new house two years ago, I still got rid of more stuff. I was unpacking and organizing the kitchen, and in doing so, I had to stop and ask myself, "Why does one person need more than thirty coffee mugs?" The answer was simple: I don't. I drink one or two cups of coffee a day, and when I have guests over, we usually drink wine, water, or beer. If my guests do drink coffee, it's usually no more than about four people. I got rid of all but six coffee mugs.

I've read a few books over the past few years about simplifying and decluttering one's life. Some of them have been great. Others have sounded great, but I knew their approaches wouldn't work for me. We all need to experiment with strategies until we find what will work for us. As unique beings, the approach that works for one person may not work well for us. That's why I'm sharing my stories and giving you my examples. You may find some inspiration in them and hopefully take some strategies from them. But in the end, hopefully you find my stories prompt you to look at areas of your life where you can make changes and tweaks that work for you.

One of the strategies I have adopted in the past few years is the rule that that nothing enters my house unless something of equal or greater size or leaves it. Admittedly, I don't always stick to that rule, but I try. Planting it into my brain has forced me to evaluate my purchases more consciously and honestly, asking myself, "Do I really need this?" Most of the time, the answer is yes because I don't shop for pleasure anymore. I shop with purpose. But inevitably, there is the odd item I see in a store that I really like and decide I want. I allow myself to buy it if I can see that what I spend will be worth it—but also if I can think of something to get rid of. Therefore, I'm replacing something with this new purchase.

NOTE:

"Nothing enters my house unless something of equal or greater size leaves it!"

When I was helping my grandpa downsize his life and move to a smaller place, we looked at the possibility of selling some of his stuff. We sold various items, but we ended up simply throwing away others, even though there were perfectly good items up for grabs. My grandpa, in his wisdom, pointed out to me that "something is only worth what someone is willing to pay for it." And he was right. I was also responsible for getting rid of my grandma's set of china. She had boxes of dishes that were "worth" hundreds of dollars because that's what she paid for them, but no one wanted them. I ended up giving them away.

Don't get caught up in the frantic push to buy "collectors" items: Beanie Babies, Cabbage Patch Kids Dolls, and other "collectibles" that people rushed out to buy and collect are not investments. You may end up spending hundreds of dollars on stuff that, years later, you end up giving away—or worse, throwing away—because no one is willing to pay anything for them. Having garage sales is a lot of work and you may make a bit of cash from your stuff, but also don't be surprised if no one wants some of your "valuable stuff." You will inevitably have people offer to pay you fifty cents for something you have marked at a dollar. If you had the same item marked at fifty cents, the same person would offer you twenty-five because people always want something for less, and what is valuable to you does not have the same value to others.

Chapter 10

Don't "invest" in stuff; buy what you need and invest in true money-making opportunities.

Treating Yourself

Treat yourself now and then, but limit your treats, especially your expensive ones. If you have a cupcake every day, then it really isn't a treat anymore; it's a habit. It's part of your routine. If you have a cupcake once every two months, then you look forward to the cupcake much more than you would if you knew you were going to have one every day.

People get excited about Christmas because Christmas comes once a year, and it's a chance to make a big deal out of a certain special event. There are Christmas songs that say, "I wish it were Christmas every day," but if that were true, then it wouldn't be special anymore. Those who do love it—not everyone does—love it so much *because* it comes once a year. We look forward to it all year, and especially in November and December as it draws near.

Ration your treats. Your pocketbook will thank you, but even more so, your psyche will appreciate them much more than if your treat were a regular part of your life.

My Story: Treating Myself!

I grew up on a cattle ranch ten minutes from the nearest town, and my parents had little money. We were largely self-sufficient. My mom grew a huge garden every year, and therefore, we had freezers full of not only vegetables but also chicken, turkey, beef, and pork, all of which we raised and butchered ourselves. My mom went to town on average once a week for supplies like toilet paper, sugar, and flour. We had a milk cow and chickens, so all of our dairy products came from the farm: eggs, milk, cream, and homemade butter, ice cream, and cottage cheese. My parents were frugal and practical because they had to be. My sister and I mainly got treats like chocolate bars, chips, and candy at Christmastime.

We also got treats when my dad went to town, which was rarely. In the summer, he would go a bit more often than in the winter if he needed machinery parts for fixing some of his farm equipment or if he was selling grain. My dad always brought us treats, usually chocolate bars. If my sister or I went to town with him, we got to have a Coke from the old-fashioned chest vending machine at the farm-equipment shop while we waited for him to do his business.

Chips and pop and chocolate bars were treats because we got them so rarely. We were excited to get them, and having these treats felt special. Even though we were young kids, we knew how tight money was, and that made our treats even more special because we knew they were paid for by hard work.

We all work hard for our money, and so treating ourselves should be part of life. "Treating" ourselves daily not only diminishes the special feeling of getting that treat, but it can also pull a lot more out of our pocketbook than we might be able afford at times.

Chapter 11 Saying No to the Upsell

How many times do you place your order for coffee or a fast-food lunch only to be asked if you want more? A burger and fries is X amount; add a drink and it's only cents more! Or a coffee is all that you wanted, but by the time you complete your order and drive away, you may have been convinced that you "need" a muffin or donut to go with that coffee. Realistically, how often do you enter a shopping situation knowing exactly what you want but when the transaction is done, you end up walking away with more? And, of course, paying more.

It's an age-old marketing trick, and so many of us fall for it. The seemingly constant push to get us to spend more by buying more when we really don't need or even want more is one of the main themes that

Morgan Spurlock pushed through in his 2004 documentary, *Super Size Me*.[14] The goal was to show whether McDonald's food was, in fact, making people sick, but he also emphasized the marketing ploy used by fast-food chains and retailers to get us to spend more on something we don't need.

In North America, the barrage of marketing messages telling us that **if we spend just a little more, we will get a lot more** has permeated not only fast food but also pretty much any retail experience. Whether you are buying a coffee or a new vehicle, the purchase will always come with the "offer" to get a good deal on a donut or an upgraded sound system or a spoiler on the back of your car. Seriously, what purpose does a spoiler serve?

Actually, a spoiler on a car is intended to reduce wind resistance thereby giving you better gas mileage when you drive. But according to Jason Tchir in the *Globe and Mail*'s October 2014 article, "Do Spoilers Actually Improve a Car's Performance?", most spoilers on vehicles these days are just for show. They don't actually improve vehicle performance, especially if most or all of your driving is at less than 100 kph. If you live in the city and always drive in the city, a spoiler is pretty much useless. And how much do they

---

[14] *Super Size Me*, directed by Morgan Spurlock (2004; Appleton, WI, United States: Roadside Attractions), DVD.

cost? Well, the most basic, simplest, and cheapest one will be under a hundred dollars. Most will be much more than that.[15] Is it worth it?

Questioning the "Deal"

Be wary of fundraisers. Sometimes they are a good deal, but a lot of products sold through school or community fundraisers are actually more expensive than they would be if you bought them on your own. The coupon books have been great deals for me because plenty of their coupons get me my money's worth and much more. As with anything, compare prices. The advantage to buying from a fundraiser is that you are also supporting an organization that might be important to you, but don't feel pressured to support it, either. If you don't need something and can't afford it, but you do want to support the cause, give a donation instead. They will be happy for your money, and you get the tax credit! You also won't get an item that you may not need or want. If you do want to support a fundraiser, take advantage of the product

---

[15] Jason Tschir, "Do Spoilers Actually Improve a Car's Performance?" *The Globe and Mail*, October 21, 2014, https://www.theglobeandmail.com/globe-drive/culture/commuting/do-spoilers-actually-improve-a-cars-performance/article21180268.

they are selling to do double duty—maybe they are selling something that your best friend would love as a birthday gift. Two birds with one stone!

Consider whether membership fees at stores such as Costco will save you enough money to make the membership worthwhile. Some items are cheaper at Costco than other stores, but others are similar in price or even more expensive. Analyze your shopping habits and calculate for yourself whether the annual Costco membership will save you money in the long run.

NOTE:

Joining multiple rewards programs means you are earning a few points here and there. Focus in on one rewards program so you accumulate points faster.

Also, joining multiple programs means you are earning a few points here and there, and it will take a long time to accumulate enough points to cash in. If you focus your efforts on one rewards program, the points will accumulate in one program, earning you rewards faster. For example, most grocery stores either

Chapter 11

have their own points programs or are affiliated with Air Miles. Choose one grocery store and make most of your purchases there, planning around sales. Friends of mine told me that when flyers come to their mailbox every Friday, they sit down and look for the groceries they need, planning out their route for Saturday. Then they visit multiple stores, buying sale items.

This may work if all the stores you plan to hit are within a few blocks of each other, but in a city as large as Calgary, consider how much time and gas money you may be spending driving between and shopping at multiple locations. Is the sale price of the veggies really worth the time and gas money? If so, great, but if not, focus all your spending on one store so that you rack up points with them faster and can therefore redeem the points for cash back. I am always thrilled when I'm at a checkout and the cashier says to me, "You have $10 credit with your points. Would you like to redeem that $10 now?" Sure, why not? Ten dollars is ten dollars! Or I may choose to leave it to climb higher. I never really keep track of my points, and so to have a cashier tell me I have a $10 dollar credit is free money!

Debt-Free at Forty-Three

My Story: Recognizing That More Is Unnecessarily More

My last few vehicles have been brand new. The only accessory I have added is the removable cover for the back of my SUV so that people wandering through a parking lot can't see what goodies I am carting around. Buying this cover a was a peace-of-mind purchase so that I can worry less about people breaking the windows of my vehicle to steal that valuable bag of rice or the books I'm taking to a Little Free Library.

As we all are, I am guilty of last-minute spontaneous purchases when I have gone into a store or coffee shop with one thing on my mind. Usually, it's the pumpkin scones in September and October from a certain coffee chain that we can all blame for starting the pumpkin latte craze! However, I've also been known to get a little mouthy at the drive-through window:

> **Me:** I'd like a burger and fries, please, and that's all.
>
> **Faceless staff worker:** Would you like to add a drink to that to make it a combo?

> **Me:** No. Just the burger and fries.
>
> **Staff worker:** Can I interest you in a muffin or a donut today?
>
> **Me:** No, *as I said twice already, that's all.*

At this point, the person taking my order is usually a little flustered. And while I haven't been rude or snarky in my tone, they are clearly taken aback by someone pointing out that they have said for the third time now that they don't want the upsell. I realize these people are simply "doing their jobs." I'm just annoyed that it's pretty much impossible to have an interaction at a fast-food or coffee chain anymore that isn't completely scripted for the sole purpose of selling me more. The "more is better" mentality has become so pervasive in our society that the person taking an order on the other side of a drive-through speaker doesn't even fully listen to your initial order. When I say "that's all" in my initial order, they persist with trying to sell me more. It's maddening.

I stopped going to home-based-business parties years ago because I found I was always walking out having ordered tons of stuff that I didn't need. When a friend invites you to a sales party they are hosting, of course you want to support them, but it's hard to leave the party without overspending. You don't want to be the person who only buys one low-priced item, or worse, the only person at the party who didn't buy anything! "I'm just here for the snacks" doesn't promote much goodwill, even with your closest of friends. They did, after all, invite you because they want the great host gift. You end up looking like the jerk who only came for the food if you don't spend a certain amount, and that certain amount can be quite high if you're not careful. I just started politely declining the invitations altogether. That way, I'm not in the position to be either the one person eating snacks and not opening my wallet or one who overspends on stuff I end up never using.

In the days of COVID-19, though, and with technology allowing us to do more remotely, I have recently been invited to more and more Facebook versions of these parties. I had been invited to one for a certain product, something I absolutely would never use and never give to anyone as a gift, and so I just declined that invitation. A recent invitation, though, was for products that I do use and like. There was one item I needed, but it was out of stock. I bought a couple of other items that I technically didn't need, but I knew the quality was good and that I would use it. Great. I supported my friend and spent a bit of money on something I know I will use and enjoy.

Chapter 11

The next morning, I got a message from the representative thanking me for my order and telling me that I was "only $47 away from free shipping" and to let her know if I wanted to add something to my order to get the free shipping. Um, when I had submitted my order the previous day, I noticed shipping was $13 and change. Now I was being told that I only had to spend $47 more in order to get the $13 shipping fee waived. Wait, what? "Free" shipping? According to my calculations, the shipping would actually cost me $47 if I went the route she was encouraging me to go instead of the $13 I had already agreed to pay. But hey, **I would get something else that I don't need** for that $47! And I would "save" money?! Nope.

Remember, these pitches are not coming at you with your needs and your best interest at play. Spending that extra $47 doesn't get you "free shipping." It gets another product sold and therefore puts more money into the coffers of the company and of the sales representative—while taking money from your wallet for something you didn't need or want in the first place. You don't owe it to this multi-billion-dollar company, or to the salesperson you will likely never see again, to spend your hard-earned money. You owe it to yourself to put **your** needs first, not theirs.

You see, a lot of us fall for this kind of ploy because that "free shipping" or "free" whatever is enticing. Surely, I could find something for $47 — maybe something that another friend could use? Or would I simply end up buying something and giving it to someone who would let it sit in their cupboard, unused, until they get rid of it years later?

These sales pitches are constantly thrown at us to make us second-guess ourselves — to make us think, "Oh wait, maybe I did forget something!" or "Maybe I do need something else" when really, we didn't and we don't. These pitches are well researched, and salespeople are trained to throw them at us knowing that there's a good chance we will catch the pitch and throw back our credit card number in response. The problem is, these pitches are thrown at us even though we didn't want to play ball to begin with. To stand there, letting the ball drop to the ground instead of catching it and throwing it back, makes us look like we're being difficult, ungrateful, or foolish for not wanting to take advantage of this "great deal." These pitches play on our guilt and FOMO — our fear of missing out.

The term *FOMO* was added to the Oxford English Dictionary in 2004 when researchers noticed heightened anxiety in people engaged in certain activities as a response to what they see on social media.[16] Think about what you see on your Facebook, Twitter, Instagram, and TikTok feeds: People doing fun stuff that you're not doing. People enjoying places you've never been to. People buying new vehicles that are nicer than yours. People sharing Instapot recipes and pictures of the great meals they made in **seconds** with their new gadget, while you cook on the stove with a dollar-store saucepan.

FOMO is just our 21st century term for the desire to "keep up with the Joneses"—always wanting to "own the same expensive objects and do the same things as your friends or neighbours, because you are worried about seeming less important socially than they are."[17] The only difference between these two terms is the context in which they originated: The "Joneses" were literally or metaphorically the people next door who had a bigger house, nicer car, and fancier lawn mower than you. These days, with the use of social media, we can see into more than just our next-door neighbour's life. What's more, the lives we

---

[16] Eric Barker, "This Is the Best Way to Overcome Fear of Missing Out," June 7, 2016, https://time.com/4358140/overcome-fomo.

[17] *Cambridge Dictionary*, s. v. "keep up with the Joneses," accessed October 26, 2020, https://dictionary.cambridge.org/dictionary/english/keep-up-with-the-joneses.

see that we perceive to be "richer" than ours drive that need to be more, do more—and, therefore, spend more.

The fact is that each of us is, and will always be, poorer than some and richer than others in terms of financial and material wealth. If you're a twenty-something college graduate with student loans entering or looking for your first career-related job, driving a clunky car, and eating off of garage sale plates, guess what? **A lot** of people your age are likely in a similar position **or worse**. People who aren't are either lucky or lying. Those of us who are older and seemingly have more may not necessarily "have" more—and even if we do, chances are pretty high that when we **were** your age, we were driving clunkers and eating with garage sale forks, too.

Several years ago, a friend who is eleven years younger than I am bemoaned the fact that I was buying something that he and his spouse could not afford. I immediately reminded him, "Yes, but I'm also eleven years older than you are; I couldn't afford this when I was your age, either." His response? "Oh." He had forgotten that small detail and instead, was focusing on what I had that he didn't.

It's easy to compare ourselves to others who have what we don't or can't have. But changing your viewpoint and looking at those who have less than you will help shift your perspective and hopefully drive down that FOMO-related anxiety. Just because someone else has it, or you can get a "good deal" on it, doesn't mean you need it.

Which brings me to my next chapter's subject: finding good deals.

Chapter 12 Looking for Deals

Advertisers want you to spend money on the products they are promoting. Sometimes sales can be great opportunities to save money, but discounts and other promotions are not necessarily always great deals.

Spending Wisely

The key to saving money on purchases is to become aware of deals, discounts, cheaper options, and sales to discern whether they really are good deals or not. Spending wisely requires a bit of time and work, but if you are on a tight budget, a little effort will help you squeeze the most out of your dollar.

You can buy a lot of items used or even get them for free. Let's take books, for example:

- Use your **library card** rather than buying books.

- Buy items such as books at **garage sales** or **community book sales** rather than buying new. The added benefit to this is that you are putting a few dollars into the pocket of an average person trying to downsize their life. You could also end up helping a charity or community organization raise some money for their operations at community sales.

- Look for a **Little Free Library** and other types of free book exchanges in your town or city. They are popping up everywhere these days! And I've found some really cool obscure books in these little nooks!

- Join **buy-and-sell groups**, **buy-nothing groups**, and similar gatherings on Facebook, Facebook Marketplace, VarageSale, etc., where you can buy, trade, or get free items that you need.

If you need something basic, buy it at a dollar store or thrift store instead of a more expensive shop.

Chapter 12

Thrift stores, in particular, are fun places to shop. They often have unique items; you never know what you will find! Most towns and cities have second-hand, consignment, or thrift shops now, and as a bonus, the money might go to a cause or charity you really want to support!

My Story: Thrifty Shopping as Part of My Social Life

I love garage sales, but I've largely stopped going to them over the years. I tend to buy stuff that I really don't need just because it's cheap or interesting. The one exception is my hometown's twice-a-year rummage sale. Every April and October, volunteers in my hometown of 3,000 people fill up the curling rink and the skating arena with donations from people who just want to get rid of stuff. The rummage sale sells almost everything: furniture, tools, games, puzzles, tchotchkes, Christmas lights and ornaments for inside and out, wrapping paper, greeting cards, books, CDs, records, clothes, dishes, quilts, fabric, craft supplies, costume jewellery, household appliances, and more. One of my favourite sections of the sale, and the place I usually hit first, is the "new" table. Local businesses and residents who are clearing out dust-collecting boxes of "treasures" may have items that have never been used. I have found "brand-new" items from the seventies, still in the box, that someone likely got as a wedding or birthday gift but never used!

This sale is a lot of fun for me. It draws people from all over town but also from other communities. I live a three-hour drive away, and I make the trek because it's a fun social event in addition to a treasure hunt. I am guaranteed to run into old family friends from my time growing up there. I'm also guaranteed to come home with a few "treasures." The prices are cheap, and there are always unique items. These days, I'm trying to downsize my life, but I can't help buying brand-new wrapping paper or gift bags for twenty-five cents each.

And books. Books will always be a weakness of mine because I love to read, and I also like to support this rummage sale because twice a year, they raise over $24,000 for the local hospital auxiliary. That alone is a good enough excuse for me to spend twenty-five cents per paperback or fifty cents per hardcover on a book I may only read once and then give away. Who can beat those prices?

Bonus Story #1: Sometimes You Just Get Lucky!

When my parents lived on their farm, my mom used to volunteer at the rummage sale. My dad, being a cattle rancher, always needed new jeans. Since he spent the majority of his time outside working with the cattle or in the field, he didn't care if some of his work jeans were new or had holes in them. My mom would always look for jeans for him at the rummage sale. As she taught me, why pay $40 or $50 or more for a new pair of jeans when you can buy a used pair, in perfectly good condition, for fifty cents—especially when your husband only uses them for working outside in the barn or field?

Well, she brought home a pair of jeans one time, in his size. Fifty cents was the going rate, so that's what she spent. Nothing wrong with these jeans at all—no holes, no stains. They had only been worn a few times. They looked new.

She threw them at Dad for him to try on, which he did. And when he did, he stuck his hands in the pockets and pulled out a five-dollar bill! That's mad profit!

Bonus Story #2: Accidental Savings

A few years ago, my dad was in the hospital for several weeks, and I went to visit him almost every day. One morning, when I pulled into the parking lot, I moved the parking receipt from the previous day off my dashboard in anticipation of paying for parking and putting the new receipt on my dash. However, for some reason, I looked at the receipt and noticed that it was good for twenty-four hours. Since I had paid $8.50

for parking the previous afternoon, my receipt was still valid! So I got "free" parking for my morning visit.

Taking Advantage of Sales

One of my life goals is to avoid paying full price for anything unless I absolutely have to. At times, I don't have a choice, but there are a lot more opportunities to save money than many people realize.

We're all told to negotiate on big purchases like a vehicle or a house, and in doing so, we can potentially save a few thousand dollars. In our society, though, we don't negotiate on smaller items such as clothing, groceries, or other items that you might barter for in markets in some countries. However, that doesn't mean you have to pay top dollar for these items, either, even if you buy them new in a non-thrift store.

Here are a few pointers on saving money on regular items:

- **Wait for times of the year when you know sales will be happening.** These include sales marketed for back-to-school, Black Friday, Boxing Week, etc.
- **Keep your eyes open for special discounts that may apply to you.** For

example, many car rental agencies, hotels, and other businesses offer 5% to 10% discounts if you are a CAA member. Teachers are honoured at teacher appreciation sales events in some stores, and if you are a government worker, you can show your government ID for discounts at places like hotels, museums, etc. Keep your eyes and ears open for student or senior discounts if you fall into one of those categories, as well.

- **Buy generic or no-name brands instead of name brands.** There can be significant price differences between name brands and the equivalent, generic brands. If the only difference you notice in the product is in the name or the price, choose the cheaper option. You can buy common generic or no-name products without sacrificing quality in the grocery store, for example.

- **Buy items like winter sports equipment or summer clothing at the end of the season** when stores want to clear out seasonal inventory.

- **Know an item's usual price** by observing what you pay over time, and determine if the sale price is a good deal or not.

- **Compare the sale price of the same item to its regular price or to a sale price in a different store.** Sometimes a sale price is no better than regular price at a cheaper store! Along with this, lots of stores and businesses do price matches, so if you are in the market for something like a printer, compare prices in different stores. If you prefer to shop at a particular store but their price is higher, see if they will match or beat the cheaper price offered elsewhere.

- **Get to know the pattern of sales in your grocery store or other stores.** Look for other store-specific promotions. Some stores such as Mark's, Fabricland, and grocery stores have sales pretty much every week or weekend. In many grocery stores, especially, the same item goes on sale every two to five weeks. Spend a few minutes looking at flyers, email updates, or websites to check out what specific items are on sale on any given day. Plan your shopping trips on days that you know will offer discounts on the items you need.

TIP:

In many grocery stores, the same item goes on sale every two to five weeks, so plan to buy certain items only when they are discounted.

Stock up on non-perishables and items with a long shelf life when they go on sale so that you don't find yourself needing something and having to pay full price at the last minute.

If you need to make a large purchase, look for promotions or discounts on large purchases, such as 0% interest on vehicle purchases—but read the fine print to ensure you truly are getting a 0% loan. Wait for sales and promotions if you can. For example:

- Spring and early summer are good times to buy vehicles; dealerships want to clear out the previous year's inventory before the new stock comes in.

- August is a great time to find back-to-school deals on laptops and other school supplies.
- Canada has adopted Black Friday in recent years, and this is a great time to buy Christmas presents or winter clothes at discount prices.

Just be sure to do your homework so that you know for a fact that you are getting a good deal. Sometimes these "sales" are what the regular prices already were or should be before a markup! And don't buy anything just because it's a good deal. If you don't need it, don't buy it. Not spending money on something saves you more money than buying it on sale.

My Story: I Never Pay Full Price for Toilet Paper

Other than the three years I spent living in Japan, I've never paid full price for toilet paper. When I was in university, my grandmother used to give me and her other grandchildren toilet paper on a regular basis. She loved buying it when it was on sale and giving it to us because she knew it was practical.

Getting Grandma's discount toilet paper became a beloved joke in our family, and I found it funny and endearing that she made a point of buying it

Chapter 12

for her grandchildren. At one point, she stopped doing this, and I was disappointed. It had become a fun tradition!

And so, I carried on the tradition for myself. As a bit of a sentimental game, I guess, I made a point of following in my grandmother's footsteps and only buy toilet paper when it goes on sale. Because I shop at the same store for all of my groceries, I quickly noticed their sale patterns: Toilet paper goes on sale for half price every three weeks. I make a point of buying one or two packages of toilet paper at a time, throwing the extra into my garage, and as a result, I never run short. I keep track of how much I have on hand and if I see I'm on the last package, I make a note to buy it the next time I see it on sale.

Toilet paper is one silly item, but why pay full price for something if you don't have to? I pay roughly $6 for a package of toilet paper when it goes on sale instead of paying $12 for full price. Six dollars plus six dollars plus six dollars … think about all the toilet paper even one person buys over the course of ten years. That's a fair bit of cash I have saved!

I've made one of my life mantras "Why pay full price for something if you don't have to?" And often you don't have to.

Another savings opportunity I have taken advantage of is when buying a turkey for Christmas or

Thanksgiving. Every grocery store has promotions during holiday seasons. For several years, my grocery store had the following promotion: If you spent $100 or more on groceries, you could get a $10 discount on your Christmas turkey, which were also on sale for 99 cents per pound. During the holiday season, in particular, it's easy to spend $100 on groceries. And since I don't feed twenty people for Christmas dinner, I always look for small turkey. Ten to twelve pounds is ideal for me and so at the sale price, my turkey would cost $10-$12. Factor in the $10 discount and I always got my turkeys for either a couple of dollars or for free! My grocery store doesn't do this anymore, and I miss my free turkeys.

Using Coupons and Member Discounts

Time is money, and so spending a great deal of time looking for sales, coupons, or discounts might not be worth it in some cases. But once you get to know patterns, you can check for deals more quickly.

- **Look for coupons in your mail, email, or newspaper**. These are becoming increasingly rare, but if you still get junk mail in your mailbox, you will find discount vouchers from time to time. Most coupons are digital, so keep your eyes open on your social media and in your email inbox, as well. Use coupons, but only if you need the product or service. Remember, you save more money by not buying products you don't need!

- **Look through coupon books that are sold for fundraisers such as Entertainment and ADmazing Savings.** If you see enough coupons that will save you the value of what you paid for the book and more, you will save yourself money as well as support the fundraising group (usually schools, children's sports teams, etc.).

- **Negotiate for extras, discounts, or bonuses when making big purchases such as a vehicle.** You're spending a lot of money, so ask the dealership to kick in some free or discounted accessories. Negotiate with them to give you a year's worth of free oil changes, for example.

- **Look for store-specific deals and promotions.** Many stores offer points programs or membership discounts because they want your loyalty as a regular customer. It's worth it to join some of these, but be selective. Choose one store where you will find what you need. There are multiple places to find hardware and home renovation supplies, and you may not necessarily find everything you need at one store. But if you choose one as your main source for shopping, join their points program and focus on spending at that store.

My Story: Streamlining

I don't have a Costco membership. As a single woman with no children, and considering what I buy, I wouldn't save enough money to justify the annual membership. (Plus, I refuse to pay for the "right" to shop at a store, but that's another issue entirely.) Instead, I look for sales at my local grocery store, which is also closer to my house than Costco anyway.

I do have the Flashfood app on my phone and I check it fairly regularly to see what's available. Used by Loblaws and other stores, Flashfood is a program that showcases grocery items that are nearing their expiry date. The grocery store is looking to sell them rather than send them to the landfill. It's a double win! You save money, and you save food from being wasted. The selection on Flashfood changes throughout the day as items sell and as the store adds new items to the app: bread, cheese, milk, nuts, candy, yogurt, hummus, pastries, meat, and produce. It also offers canned goods that may be nearing their lifespan. The grocery items are half price or less. You simply pay, reserve the items on the app, and go pick them up in person. Every now and then, I buy bananas at a huge discount. As a single person, I don't eat a lot of bananas over the course of a couple of days, but for five dollars, I can put three large plastic bags in my freezer that I can quickly grab and thaw to use for smoothies or muffins.

I do volunteer costume design for community theatre. Because the theatre group is non-profit, those of us who do costume design try to find discounted fabric, lace, trim, and even thread to save the organization money. I often stop at thrift stores when I'm driving by to see their new stock, and I have found some really great fabrics for a fraction of the price that I would pay at a fabric store. Not to mention, sometimes I find unique fabrics that I wouldn't be able to find anywhere else. Happy accidents!

When I was on a two-week tour of Egypt with a friend a couple of years ago, I was smack in the middle of designing costumes for a show. My designs were finalized, and I knew what supplies I needed. I had already done some shopping, and so I had a good idea of what I had and what I needed. While on the top deck of our cruise ship, sailing down the Nile, sitting beside the swimming pool relaxing, I got on my phone and took a peek at Facebook Marketplace.

Suddenly I started giggling and my travel companion asked, "Ok, what are you up to now?"

I gleefully told him, "I just bought some fabric for *Cabaret*."

"HERE?" he replied?

I confirmed, "Well, it's in Calgary, so I can pick it up when we get home, but I just nabbed it from here right now, yes."

After that, because of Facebook's algorithms, I started getting "You might like" notifications from Facebook of cool fabrics that were for sale through Facebook Marketplace and were available in Luxor, Cairo, and other nearby towns and cities. Sadly, I didn't buy any fabric in Egypt, much as I would have liked to, but I did buy some neat stuff from home while I was in the middle of the Nile. And it was cheap.

Chapter 13 Maximizing Your Tax Situation

Doing Your Taxes

I'm a huge fan of trying to pull back as much payable income tax every year as possible.

First things first, though: Start by ensuring that you **file your taxes every year, and file them on time.** Your employer should hopefully be taking enough money off of your paycheque that you won't have to pay extra taxes. But on the chance that you do owe more, make sure you file your taxes before the deadline. Then pay any outstanding balance before late fees and penalties kick in. These fees and penalties are high, and they are wasted money.

IMPORTANT:

File your taxes every year, and file them on time.

A lot of people are intimidated by the idea of doing their taxes. I actually love it. Why? I'm not a math whiz; it's not the calculations that I love. What I loved as a teacher was the fact that I almost always got a refund of at least a couple hundred dollars. Now that I'm self-employed, I have to figure out how much to pay, but I still love the challenge of trying to get out of paying as much tax as possible—legally, of course. If you are getting a refund, why would you delay getting it? Get your money back from the government as soon as possible so that **you** can use it. Why let them keep money that is yours even a day longer than possible?

Also, I suspect most people agree with me here: Why let the government have any more of your money than necessary? There are lots of tax deductions and exemptions available. The trick is knowing what they are and making sure you take advantage of them. If your financial situation is quite simple, then doing your own taxes with software such as TurboTax is quick, straightforward, and cheap. And TurboTax allows you to do a rough estimate well ahead of time. This way, you'll get a sense of whether you need to pay

Chapter 13

or whether putting more into your RRSPs will help you get more of a refund.

If your taxes are more complicated than most, don't be afraid to hire a good accountant to complete and file them for you. It's money well spent. For a few hundred dollars, an accountant may be able to get you a bigger tax refund than you are able to squeeze out for yourself because they know more tricks and deductions.

Regardless of whether you are doing your taxes yourself or an accountant is doing them for you, knowing how to maximize your deductions helps you keep more money when it comes to paying your taxes.

Claiming Tuition

Tuition is tax deductible, so any time you take a course—whether it's related to your career or not—be sure to claim the tuition. I have taken a number of undergraduate courses through the years for my own interest. They haven't been required for my job or done much to further me in my career. However, they have helped sharpen my brain and enhance my research, writing, and referencing skills—as well as being really fascinating, to boot! And they are tax deductible. I may not go to movies as often as some people, but life-long learning is a priority for me. If you are interested in learning about anything just for fun, take a course and claim the tuition on your taxes!

Claiming RRSP Contributions

Having devoted a whole chapter to investments and RRSP accounts, I won't go into a lot of detail here. However, I want to reiterate that whatever you put into your RRSP every year gives you roughly a 30% credit on your income tax. If you put $1,000 in, you'll get around a $300 credit—which means that if you owe taxes, your RRSP contributions can reduce the amount that you still owe. If you are getting a refund, RRSP contributions can add to it. So put as much into your RRSPs as you can. Not only will you get a bigger tax refund (or at least reduce the amount you still owe), but your RRSP contributions will grow over time in a tax-sheltered investment.

Claiming Deductions for Working from Home

If you work at home, a lot of tax deductions are available to you: portions of your utilities, office supplies, etc. If you are self-employed and drive for work, you can claim gas and mileage. Aas mentioned, I hire an accountant to manage my taxes for me. The math on this kind of stuff makes my brain hurt, but if you are good at accounting, look at what you can deduct for these expenses and claim them.

If your brain hurts trying to figure this stuff out, too, hire an accountant. It really doesn't cost terribly much to have a professional do your taxes for you. I swear by the adage "You have to spend money in order to make money." It's entirely possible that the money you pay an accountant will be worth it. Ideally, they will identify tax credits that you don't know are available or can't figure out how to include in your tax return.

Claiming Child Care and Other Child-Related Expenses

I don't have kids. I don't even have nieces or nephews, so admittedly, I'm no expert on raising kids. I *am* a "self-appointed auntie" for my friends' kids, and so I know a wee bit about how expensive kids are and what kinds of tax deductions and benefits are available for parents. Find out what the exemptions are—child care, medications for your children, etc.—and grab onto those benefits. Also, if you can afford it, open an RESP account for your kid(s) as soon as possible.

Check the CRA website to see what child tax benefits you qualify for, and if you are confused, ask your accountant to find and maximize these credits for you.

Claiming Health Expenses

Keep your receipts for any health-related expenses you incur each year. If you have health benefits that cover your prescriptions, dental work, etc., that's great. But even so, keep receipts for anything you pay out of pocket. You can claim these expenses, too, if they total a minimum amount. Anything that your health benefits don't cover qualifies: deductibles and remaining balances for prescriptions, hospital parking fees, meals and fuel related to travel for medical care, etc. Keep **all** receipts so you have proof that you've incurred the expense. If your accountant tells you that a certain expense doesn't qualify, so be it. But it's better to have the receipt and not need it than the other way around—and thus miss out on a tax deduction.

TIP:

Keep all receipts for health and business-related expenses.

Chapter 13

Claiming Charitable Donations

Unfortunately, many of us have funerals to attend now and then. Our deceased friend or family member may have succumbed to an illness. Maybe a non-profit organization in your community or in the world was important to them. When you attend a funeral, most of the time, a notice will be printed that in lieu of flowers, donations to a non-profit organization chosen by the deceased person or their family would be appreciated. If you wish to do so, by all means, donate. Likewise, if a non-profit or a charitable organization has significance to *you*, donate to them.

A tax receipt is issued for a $20 minimum donation to any registered charity or non-profit organization. Even a small donation will give you a little bit of money back on your tax return while also contributing to a cause that is special to you.

If money is tight, you probably don't give much or anything to charitable organizations. If you do, however, these donations are great tax deductions. The return on your donation is roughly 30% of what you donate.

Claiming Professional Development (PD) Expenses

If you are paying for PD other than courses, look for ways to get tax deductions for it, too. Even better, see if you can get the cost of the PD covered by your employer! Many workplaces and professional organizations have funds set aside for PD. Check to see if your employer or union has such funds available. If so, they may pay for most or all of the cost of a conference. If your workplace requires you to attend a conference, it should be paying the cost anyway! But if you hear of an interesting conference, webinar, or workshop that you choose to attend, see if you can get your employer to cover the cost. If nothing else, claim the expense on your tax return.

If you're taking a university course or an entire degree or diploma, look for grants and scholarships. There are a lot out there!

My Story: Donating What I Would Have Spent Anyway

My mom died young. So did a close friend of mine. I felt cheated because both of these people theoretically should have been in my life for decades longer than they were.

Chapter 13

Every year, I donate the amount of money I would have spent on Christmas presents for these two people to charities in their name. My reasons for this are twofold: to honour their memory, and to support causes that are now important to me because they were important to my mom and my friend. I could keep back that money, but it's a sentimental gift to these organizations and part of my grieving and remembering them. And these donations are also tax deductions.

Chapter 14 Finding Money

Sometimes you find money. I mean, sometimes you literally find money, like nickels or quarters on the ground. I know it makes me look like a cheapskate, but I always pick up money when I see it on the ground! Usually it's a few cents, but I've also found $20 bills just sitting on the pavement in front of me. I always wonder if it's a trick—like the *Just for Laughs* gags when the TV show producers put a $20 bill on the ground attached to a string. Someone then pulls the string when a passerby bends to pick it up so that they can film you looking silly. My found money has never had strings attached.

While you may not become a millionaire by picking up abandoned quarters on the ground, pick them up. Every cent counts. You know what they say about a drop in the bucket—it takes many, many drops of water to make an ocean, but with enough drops, you eventually get there. Money is money. Don't walk past free money.

What I call "found money" also includes gifts, inheritances, bonuses from your job, and perks from your rewards programs. As a teacher, I never got cash bonuses, but some companies and organizations do give bonuses as commission, incentives, or thank-you gestures at year-end. Inheritances are something you have no control over, but you may be the recipient of one at some point. Likewise, sometimes you receive monetary gifts for birthdays, Christmas, other occasions, or "just because." Someone may give you a thank-you gift in the form of a gift card; that's free money!

When I receive a gift card from someone, my first instinct is to immediately start to brainstorm what kind of treat I can buy for myself with the card. Most people's minds probably instinctively go this route. Treating yourself now and then is important, and certainly the person giving you the card likely meant for you to treat yourself, but you can also be practical with these gift cards. If the gift card is for Amazon, you can put the card toward a new gadget or book, or you can be practical and order that new pair of shoes that you desperately need for work. If you needed to buy the shoes anyway, having someone hand you a gift card that you can use for that purchase is bonus money.

Chapter 14

Taking Advantage of Rewards Programs

We've all been cautioned about putting all of our eggs into the same basket, and in many situations, this is good advice. However, when it comes to rewards programs, the opposite is true.

Take a look at how many cards you have in your wallet for different loyalty programs. Practically everywhere you shop has a customer loyalty program, offering you discounts, freebies on your birthday, and points you can redeem for cash or products. Consider your shopping needs and what types of stores you frequent. We all need groceries. If you have a new home, you likely visit some home renovation or gardening stores as you build a fence, deck, garage, garden, or flower plot. We need clothes, and we put gas in our vehicles. What other types of products or services do you frequently spend money on?

Perhaps there are huge price differences saving you significant amounts of money by shopping in different grocery stores and capitalizing on each one's deals. However, it more likely makes sense to join the rewards program of one business or chain. Not all rewards programs are created equally. With the same discerning eye that you use to choose a credit card, look at what perks you get from different loyalty programs. Focusing on one rewards program will speed up the time it takes to both rack up points and get you greater rewards than spreading your spending between multiple programs will. One hundred points in one program rather than fifty points across two programs means you can redeem those points sooner.

Also look for double-dipping opportunities. For example, if both your grocery store and your credit card offer rewards points, pay for your groceries with that card. You'll accumulate points in both programs, thereby making your grocery purchases worth twice as much.

Finding Travel Deals

As I mentioned earlier, some credit cards or other rewards programs, such as Air Miles, can earn you perks for travel. I travel a lot, so this is one area where I am always looking to save some money to maximize my experience.

In addition to credit card perks, you can also find good deals through airline and accommodation bookings. Every airline has a rewards program. Increasingly more airlines offer different levels of ticketing, depending on whether you want cancellation or rebooking options, baggage fees included, or priority boarding, for example. You can get good deals on air tickets if you look for seat sales and buy basic fares.

Chapter 14

I've been booking all of my hotels through Hotels.com for years because the prices are the same, or sometimes cheaper, than other sites. What's more, for every ten nights you stay at a place through a Hotels.com booking, you get a free night's accommodation that is worth the average of the ten nights. They have different status levels, too, so if you travel a lot, you can earn better perks and get access to their "secret" prices.

My Story: Take the Deal

For reasons that I don't understand, the longer your flight itinerary, the cheaper it is. You would think that taking three flights and flying all over the North American continent would be more expensive than taking a direct flight. After all, you are using more gas and more people have to staff the airplanes to get you from Point A to Point B. But the airlines seem to like to reward passengers for inconveniencing them.

When I was moving back from Japan, the school I had been working for paid for my return trip home. I was responsible for buying my own ticket, but they gave me the equivalent of $1,500 for the ticket. By this time, I had done enough travelling from Tokyo to know that the milk run is by far the cheapest option. So, I took my $1,500, bought a $700 plane ticket taking me from Tokyo to Los Angeles to San Francisco to

Spokane to Calgary and pocketed the rest. My itinerary included more than thirty hours of hours travel time compared to the $1,400 ticket that would have taken me from Tokyo through Vancouver to Calgary in about fourteen hours. Inconvenient, yes. Profitable, yes. I was twenty-five and didn't care about getting home faster. I could sleep on the plane and once I got home.

Several years later, I was coming home to Canada after a vacation in Germany. I had used my airline points to get the flight for free, so I was already enjoying a cheaper vacation. While I was sitting at the airport in Frankfurt waiting for my direct flight home to Calgary, the airline staff called for volunteers to give up their seats. The flight was overbooked, and they were looking for a handful of people to relinquish their seats and take a different route home: Frankfurt to Toronto and then on to Calgary. This option would mean arriving in Calgary five hours later than the direct flight, and the airline was offering an option of either a flight voucher (good for a year) or an $800 cash payment. I took the cash, called my friend who was meeting me at the Calgary airport, told her I would be home five hours later than originally planned, and pulled out a book to read.

If options like this come up, take them when you can. I actually made money on that vacation to Germany because I was visiting friends and didn't have to pay for accommodations. My flight had been free to begin with, and in the end, the airline paid me $800 to redirect my flight home.

Generating More Income

Don't we all have an awful lot of stuff in our houses or apartments that we don't need? When I moved two years ago after living in the same house for twelve years, I took three truckloads of stuff to the landfill and eight vehicle loads of stuff to my favourite thrift store. I would have tried to sell more of my belongings to generate some income from it, but I simply didn't have time. My house sold in three days, and so instead of having two or three months to get organized and move, I had three weeks. I downsized in a hurry because I knew I had a lot of stuff I wanted to get rid of and just didn't have the time to try to connect with people and sell it. The thrift store was happy to see me. Eight times.

If you do have the time, though, go through your house. Start with one room at a time and organize your belongings into stuff you really need, stuff you want, and stuff you know you can get rid of without giving it another thought. Get rid of the last batch. Take advantage of free advertising on sites like Kijiji, Facebook, and VarageSale. As my dad said when he and my mom were organizing machinery and household items for their farm auction sale, "It's junk and it takes up space." But someone else may want your junk enough to pay you a few dollars for it. "One man's junk is another man's treasure?" You bet! I have had several garage sales over the years, and it always amazes me what people buy. Likewise, I'm surprised at what people *don't* buy! Get rid of stuff you don't need and get some cash for it if you can.

My Story: Selling Rocks

When I was moving, a lot of what I took to the thrift store and especially the landfill was stuff I had tried to sell at a garage sale or two—or stuff I knew no one would buy at a garage sale anyway. My thrift store donations were perfectly good items, and I could have gotten some money out of some of them, but as I said, I didn't have the time to try and sell anything. Any items that were broken or so dated that no one would want them went to the landfill. But the stuff I donated to the thrift store was clean and usable. It just didn't have much value, at least not to me. I felt that the time and energy required to make a few dollars out of it wasn't worth what little time and energy I had when I was packing up to move. One thing I did get the movers to bring to my new place was nine five-gallon pails of landscaping rock.

Landscaping rock is expensive, and this was still "new." I mean, it's not like I went through my backyard before I moved, skimming a top layer of rock off so that I could take some rock with me! The nine pails of rock were left over from when I initially landscaped my front and backyard. I had just never gotten around to trying to sell them, and now that the pressure was on, I didn't want to give them away. I knew I could get some money out of them, so they moved with me and then sat in my garage for another eight months until I finally got tired of looking at them. I placed an ad for them on Facebook Marketplace one Sunday morning, and about an hour later received a message from a guy saying he would take them and could come right away. Less than two hours after posting about them, I had gotten rid of a pile of rocks that took up a lot of space, and I had $90 more in my bank account. He made the e-transfer from his cellphone while standing in the back of my garage after loading the rock into his truck. Gotta love technology. He was happy, and I was happy.

Generating Passive Income

There are only twenty-four hours in a day, and, therefore, the amount of time we can spend making money is limited. Even if you work an eighty-hour week (ugh, I hope you don't), there is a limit to how much money you can earn if you are paid by the hour or by the project.

When money is tight, our first response is to try to figure out how we can earn more. The problem might not be how much we make, though. Instead, look for ways you can spend less, especially if your earning power is limited. In short, you need to live within your means. If you are constantly trying to earn more, working yourself to death in the process, you will not have the time or energy to enjoy any extra money you end up earning, anyway.

Maybe you *are* struggling to make enough money, though, and you've cut back on your spending as much as you possibly can without resorting to living on rice and water. You can look for ways to earn more money—and earning passive income won't kill you off in the process.

Passive income refers to any money you generate without much or any effort. Your work at your job is not passive; you are actively working to obtain that money. Finding a fifty-dollar bill on the street is passive. You have done nothing to acquire that money other than pick it up and pocket it.

You're not going to find tons of money laying around on the street, but there are multiple types of passive income that you can consider.

Chapter 14

Here are a few ideas:

- Share your skills or knowledge with others. Write a course, or two, or three, to offer online. Then, anytime someone takes the course, they pay you. The course doesn't have to be live. For example, my friend and editing colleague, Kimmy Beach, has a course for authors who want a bit of extra guidance on how to edit their own writing: "Editing your own prose." She wrote the course, put it on her website, and blam! Anytime anyone takes the course, she earns from it.

- **Find something to sell**. I will not attend your home party, but lots of people take on selling these home-based businesses like Pampered Chef, Scentsy, etc., to make some extra money. These days, you can take orders online as a representative for these companies without having to host a house party. Once people know you are a rep for a particular product, they can purchase online anytime without you having to do anything, and you earn a commission from their purchase. It will take a while to build a client base with these types of businesses, but if this is your thing, give it a shot and stick with it for a few years. If it's not worth your time and effort, you can always quit.

- **Build or update your website with affiliate links and paid ads.** You'll get paid for traffic to your website!

- **Sell stuff for other people online.** Lots of people have possessions they are trying to get rid of and some people don't have the time, interest, or expertise to sell online. Tap into opportunities to sell their stuff for them for a commission. (This isn't entirely passive as you still have to invest the time, but if you are good at selling online, it might be a great way to make some extra money.)

- **Get a roommate.** Having someone pay half of your rent or mortgage would be a huge help.

- **Rent your place out on Airbnb while you travel**, or participate in house swaps or exchanges to cut down on accommodation costs.

Chapter 14

- **Find the best investments for you** so that you earn money on the money you have socked away. I have specific funds that pay me guaranteed returns both monthly and annually.

Chapter 15 Using Unexpected Income

Besides finding the odd quarter lying on the ground, you may be lucky enough to find yourself on the receiving end of some unexpected income. Whether it be an inheritance, winnings from a contest or lottery ticket, a gift, or a bonus at work, unexpected income is always a nice surprise. If you work in the service industry, tips are likely part of your income—but the amounts may not necessarily always be predictable, and **you do have to claim your tips on your income tax return**. Don't try to cheat here; the CRA will find you!

It doesn't happen often, and you certainly can't count on it, but every once in a while, there's a news story about a restaurant diner leaving a hefty tip– $1,000, for example, on a dinner that cost $100. The chances of cashing in on a tip like this, a lottery or casino jackpot, or a life-changing inheritance are fairly slim, but these events do happen. And as I mentioned before, you may get smaller amounts as gifts from time to time.

If you find yourself coming into a nice chunk of surprise cash, what would you do with it? Pay down your credit card debt? Put it toward your mortgage? Blow it on a sports car? You don't necessarily need to have a game plan because something like this may not ever happen to you.

If it does happen, though, what you do with it will likely depend on where you are with your finances at that particular point in life. You may have hundreds of thousands of dollars in student loan debt and your first mortgage. Or you may have only $10,000 left to pay on your house and you are two years away from a retirement pension. Regardless, unexpected cash is a nice surprise, and if you get your hands on some, think before you act. How much it is and what you do with it could have a huge ripple effect.

My Story: Scholarships

When I was in my last year of high school, I debated where to go for university. I was a small-town kid and an introvert. The thought of going to "the big city" (Calgary) for my teaching degree scared me. I weighed two other options.

One option was to do my first two years in a small-town college and then transfer to Calgary, Lethbridge, or Edmonton to finish my teaching degree. This college accepted me and offered me a $200 music scholarship based on my application. That $200 alone was enticing because money was tight for me and at that time, $200 would have paid half my tuition for one semester. (Yes, I'm that old!) That $200 was almost the deciding factor. In the end, I decided I didn't want to settle in somewhere only to move to a different city two years later, especially when I was already accepted at one of the universities I would later transfer to. I figured it would just be simpler to go to that university to begin with and do my whole four years there.

Walking away from that $200 scholarship was tough, but in a strange turn of events, I ended up unexpectedly getting that much money anyway. Shortly after I started university in September, I was notified of the scholarship ceremony at my high school for the previous year's graduates. I was surprised to have been invited. I hadn't applied for any scholarships from my high school, but I was invited, so I went. I had no idea that at that ceremony I was going to be presented with cheques for totalling $200. I received awards for top marks in my Grade 12 TYPING class! I also received a "personality award."

Yep, I got $100 for being a nice kid!! (Apparently, my teachers thought I was, anyway .... They had nominated me for the award.)

In the end, I got the equivalent of what I had walked away from. It was money I hadn't even sought. I had no idea these awards existed, but my teachers made sure I got the cash!

Bonus Story: Miss Oblivious Gambler 2012

This is one of my favourite stories about my varied life experiences. I call this one "Miss Oblivious Gambler 2012."

I go to Vegas a few times a year. It's fun, and it's a short flight from where I live, near Calgary. Flights to Vegas from Calgary are pretty reasonable, and there's lots to do when you get there. It's my go-to place if I just need a getaway for a few days and want to hang out by a pool, have a nice meal or two, or take in some great entertainment.

In the summer of 2012, I decided that I wanted to take a road trip into the U.S. I live a little more than two hours from the Montana border, and I had a fairly new vehicle. I got the urge to see Yellowstone National Park, which I had been to once back when I was about seven or eight years old. I wanted to see it again through adult eyes.

Chapter 15

I have a cousin who lives in Wyoming whom I had never met, but we had connected through Facebook and gotten to know each other a little bit. I thought I would pop by to meet her and her husband for the first time. Well, plans for a short afternoon visit with my long-lost cousin quickly turned into the two of us planning to drive to Colorado and hop a short flight to Vegas for a three-day trip.

When I arrived at her house on a Saturday afternoon, I was welcomed with open arms by this woman and her husband I had never met. "Cousin!" she exclaimed as she grabbed me for a big hug. "Cousin-in-law!" her husband greeted me with an equally big hug. I immediately liked them and felt welcome. I could tell this was going to be a fun sub-trip of my vacation.

The next day, my cousin and I left on the three-hour drive to the airport, caught our little plane, and headed to Vegas. We were staying off The Strip in a hotel I had never heard of, but it was my cousin's chosen place and a nice resort. We checked into our rooms, had a bite to eat, and settled in to play on the slot machines.

Years ago, my mom had taught me how to use a slot machine. I remember being at the Calgary Stampede one year and Dad and I wanted to go see the animal barns. Mom was hot and tired, so she headed to the casino while waiting for us. She had gotten a taste of gambling when she and my dad had gone to Vegas years earlier for the National Rodeo Finals, and for some reason, she seemed to always have a bit of luck. She was responsible, setting her limit at $20, but more often than that, she would walk away from the machines with $40 or more—a good return on her "investment."

When Dad and I were done at the animal barns, we went to find Mom in the casino and sat down beside her. She was up a little bit of money. While I sat on the chair beside her, she looked at me, patted me on the arm and said, "I'm going to teach you how to gamble." And she did. She showed me how the slot machines worked and how much more fun it was to pull the lever of the "one-armed bandit" than to just hit the button.

By the time I caught the flight to Vegas with my cousin in 2012, I had been to Vegas two or three times myself—enough to know I loved it. The lights, the buzz, and the whole vibe is really fun for me, although I do get tired of it after about three days. That's my limit for time. For money? My limit in the casinos in Vegas is $100 a day because I figure, hey, it's Vegas. Even though you don't have to gamble to have fun there, that's part of the program.

Chapter 15

When we finished dinner, my cousin wanted to show me around the casino floor. If you've never been to Vegas, the casino sections of the hotels are huge; they can be really confusing. Word on the street is that's intentional so that you get trapped or lost and end up spending more time—and, of course, money—on the casino floor. My cousin started us off in the penny slot area, and we played a little. Then we moved on and up. By the time we got to the dollar slots, I was up between $200 and $300 dollars! One machine paid me a $75 return on my $100 deposit, and then next paid me over $150! It seemed that almost every slot machine I chose wanted to pay me a decent amount of money!

We moved to a new location and my cousin said to me, "You don't have to play here if the dollar slots are too high for you. Don't feel like you have to play just because I am." I figured, "Ah, what the heck—I'm up a few hundred dollars only a handful of hours into our vacation, and I'm here to have fun. Let's see what happens." Worst-case scenario, I would lose my winnings plus the $100 I started with, but I could always quit before I got to that point.

I chose a machine, and my cousin sat down about three machines away from me. I started to play, and after about six or seven spins, my machine stopped. It just died. I couldn't believe what I was looking at: 10X pay—7—10X pay. I looked at the little picture chart thingy on my machine and that combination wasn't on there. The closest picture to what was on my machine was 7—7—7, which paid $100, so I was confused.

Math is not my strong suit, and I just couldn't be bothered to try and figure out how much I had just won. I was surprised that the machine had just *died*—it went silent. And dark. Eerie. In the movies, when people win big, all kinds of bells and whistles and lights and sirens go off. This didn't happen, and so I thought, "Well, I've won some money, but it can't be *that* big of a deal if my machine has gone silent." All I knew at that time was that if you win more than around $200 or $300 at a machine at home in Calgary, you have to wait and be paid by the attendant. I also knew that that threshold was higher in the U.S., and so I assumed I had won several hundred dollars. As I sat waiting, I thought to myself, "Boy, if this works out to be around $700 or $800, wouldn't that be great?!" I quietly sat, patiently waiting to be paid.

As I sat there, nonchalantly looking around, quietly and patiently waiting, the young security guard, George, came to talk to me. He was a pleasant young man and started by asking where I was from, how long I'd been in town. "Do you come here often?"-type chatter. I told him I was there with my cousin and pointed her out to him. She kept looking over every now and then while playing her machine, giggling, and just checking on what was happening with me. George

Chapter 15

and I chatted for a few minutes, and then he scuttled off. Several minutes later he came back. No one else had come yet. We chatted some more. He had been in the U.S. Army for a few years and was now working security at this resort. He explained that it took the staff a while to come and pay me because of the process they had to undergo, checking the cameras to see if I had tinkered with the machine and such. I agreed politely and assured him I was fine to wait.

Finally, he looked at me quizzically and asked me, "Ma'am, do you know how much money you have won?" It must have been bothering him this whole time how calmly and quietly I was waiting.

"No," I replied. "I'm just waiting for them to come and pay me. I have no idea how much it is. My machine shut down completely and it's not telling me how much I won—maybe a few hundred dollars?"

He looked at me wide-eyed and said with a bit of a smirk on his face, "Ma'am, you've won $10,000."

I frowned at him. "NO!" I said. "There's no way."

"Yes, ma'am. You've won $10,000," he repeated, as he pointed to an itty-bitty, teeny-tiny black screen above my left knee where the words, "Jackpot Winner $10,000" were scrolling.

The moment I saw that number, I leapt out of my chair SCREAMING, **"HOLY ****!!!!! HOLY ****!!!!"** over and over. Well, that drew a crowd. And it made my cousin laugh so hard she almost fell out of her chair.

George was laughing heartily, as well, by now. It took several minutes before I calmed down and assured him that I had had no idea how much I had won until he showed me the screen ... as if I needed to clarify that! He was almost as happy for me as I was for myself and probably quite relieved that this wacky Canadian woman actually *was* excited to win the $10,000 jackpot.

Several other staff members finally came by with loads of paperwork. I had already known that if you win more than around $1,100 or $1,200 in one shot it is considered taxable income in the U.S. In Canada, casino, bingo, and lottery winnings are not taxable—but in the U.S., they are, and so my $10,000 was immediately whittled down to $7,000. The casino needed my ID, and a lovely older gentleman in a nice suit came by carrying a clipboard with all of the paperwork. Once he saw I was from Canada, he explained the tax implications to me. Of course, that was a bit of a bummer, but the reality was, I was still going home with $7,000 in my pocket, and $7,000 in U.S. dollars was going to work out to around $10,000

Canadian dollars, anyway. Nothing to complain about at all!

The man with the clipboard took my ID and disappeared. Again, I had to wait a while, and again, George kept me occupied.

Clipboard Guy finally came back, returned my ID, and told me they were still processing the payment. He gave me a copy of the tax documents, and then it occurred to me that I should now use my common sense. I asked him if they were going to be paying me in cash or if it was possible to get them to cut me a cheque. He assured me that that was my choice; if I wanted a cheque, he could let the office know and that's what I would get.

I am way too practical and sensible to not make the decision I made. Even though my adrenalin was still sprinting throughout my body, I had enough rational thought in my brain to realize that:

> A. I had just caused a huge scene, so a lot of people around me now knew that I was going to be walking away from that machine with a wad of money. I didn't want to risk being mugged before I even got back to my hotel room, where I could put the money in the safe.

> B. If I took the winnings in cash, there was also a good chance I would lose my senses and end up wasting a pile of it away in the casinos. I mean, at this point, we were only four hours into our three-day trip. We had a lot of Vegas in front of us.

I asked for the cheque and they obliged.

When I got back home to Canada, my first stop, even before I went to my house, was at my bank, where I promptly deposited the cheque. I also immediately made an appointment to see my investment adviser at the bank to arrange for that $7,000 to go into my RRSPs. I was going to get my $3,000 back; the Canadian Revenue Agency giveth what the IRS taketh away.

And so, yes, the $7,000 U.S. dollars worked out to almost $10,000 Canadian, and after putting that into my RRSP, I got another $3,000 back on my income tax for that year.

Oh, and I never did make it to Yellowstone on that trip.

Chapter 16 Taking Risks with Your Money

Here's where I insert my "Don't try this at home!" disclaimer.

I'm going to get into some high-risk activities here—financially high-risk, not sword swallowing or anything like that! You may not have the stomach for what I'm about to talk about, particularly if money is really tight. But some of us have a higher risk tolerance than others, and high risk can equal high reward. *Can*—not a guaranteed *will*. If you've got nerves of steel, read on. If you don't, you can read on anyway, but you might want to put your bank card away so that you aren't tempted to get yourself into a precarious situation.

Yes, I play the stock market—a bit. I'm no expert, but as I've grown older and gotten a bit more financial freedom, I have learned to have fun with my money. I enjoy the challenge of seeing where my limits are and trying to push them a bit further.

Admittedly, the stock market scares me because I've heard enough stories over the years of people losing their life savings that I approach it with a great deal of caution. But there are also some once-in-a-while opportunities that are pretty obvious.

I watch the news daily, and so I know what's going on in the world, including the business world. The political and social worlds are quite connected to the financial world, and at times, you can capitalize on world events.

For example, several years ago, a certain German auto manufacturer was publicly spanked good and hard for cheating on emissions tests. When I heard about this scandal, I also heard that this company's stock had plummeted. Until that moment, I had never intended on even looking at the stock market because I figured it would take a master's degree in *Something I Know Nothing About*. However, this was a really reputable company with years in operation. Their product was good, and I knew this public shaming would be temporary.

I learned how to set up a trading account through my online banking, and I bought a couple thousand dollars' worth of stock in this company. Sure

Chapter 16

enough, after a few months, the company rebounded and redeemed themselves, and I made a good batch of cash. I had set my sights on doubling my money if possible, and that's exactly what I did. As soon as my investment reached that point, I bailed. I sold all of the stocks I had bought and took the profit.

March 2020—hello, COVID-19. The month that life as we knew it stopped cold. We all shuttered in our homes. People lost their jobs. Fear and dread ensued. And the economy crashed.

"Buy low, sell high." Remember this phrase? Anyone who had some money kicking around in March 2020 had some great "sales" to take advantage of on the stock market. It was an excellent time to "buy low." Some of the companies I heard about on the news lost anywhere between 30% and 70% of their value on the NYSE.[18] Cruise ship companies and Las Vegas casinos, for example, were especially hard hit. Guess what I did?

Here's my logic: Las Vegas had shut down **COMPLETELY**. Vegas is one of the top tourist destinations in the world and surely always will be. After doing a little research, and knowing what I

---

[18] Demitrios Kalogeropoulos, "Why Royal Caribbean Stock Dove 60% in March," Nasdaq, April 2, 2020, https://www.nasdaq.com/articles/why-royal-caribbean-stock-dove-60-in-march-2020-04-02.

already know about Vegas, I chose one of the major casino chains and bought stocks. Their stock price had dropped 65% in only a few days in March 2020. I didn't get in right at the lowest point, but in looking at the history of their stock prices, I figured I had a good chance of eventually doubling my money.

Cruises were halted worldwide, so I did the same with one of the major cruise companies. There is a certain segment of society who loves cruising, including lots of people I know who only vacation on cruise ships, so again, I took a risk. I gambled on the prediction that once COVID-19 was under control—and especially once a working vaccine was at play—cruise vacations would resume and the stock prices would jump. Again, I missed getting in at the lowest point, but I estimated I could potentially double or even triple my money based on their price history.

A few months after I invested in these two stocks, I got a little nervous from the volatility I had been seeing over the summer and the fact that the pandemic was starting to drag on longer than anyone had anticipated. I sold a third of my casino shares for a 34% return. But I held on to the other two-thirds and to the cruise stock. Two months later, I sold the rest of the casino stocks for a 54% return on the day that Pfizer announced a 90% success rate for its vaccine in Stage 3 trials. The stock markets went berserk at that announcement, and I made good money that day.

Chapter 16

I have since sold all of these stocks for an average return of 50%. I could have held on to them for longer, but as the pandemic dragged on and cruises in particular were still halted, I decided not to be greedy. Instead, I opted to cash in on a sure thing. A 50% return on an investment over less than a year is *great* profit, so I took it and walked away. Since selling these stocks, their prices have risen slightly higher, but I choose not to see this as losing out and instead focus on the gains I did get.

I'm not encouraging anyone to gamble on the stock market. It has the potential to be dangerous. Very dangerous. I don't know enough about it to be a steady investor in straight stocks, but if that's of interest to you, do your research and again, get advice from experts. The stock market is quite a different bird than investing in, say, mutual funds through your RRSPs or TFSA. So unless you have good knowledge of how to trade in the markets, it's probably wise to stay away from it entirely.

Whatever your pleasure is, do spend a bit of fun money now and then on a relaxing vacation, a nice meal out, or a great new outfit. You work hard for your money, and hopefully you've got it working hard for you, so enjoy it within your means.

Conclusion

My friend Ken still teases me, thirty years after the fact, that "When Lorna needed money for tuition in university, she sold a cow." While this isn't entirely true, his teasing is based on fact.

When I was a child, my grandparents gave each of their grandkids Christmas money every year, and my mom marched my sister and me straight into the bank to put that money into an investment. I had a few hundred dollars saved even before I had finished elementary school. At that time, Mom had us putting our money into Canada Savings Bonds, which were paying in the ballpark of 10% interest yearly. My sister and I couldn't touch that money for years because it was locked in for a specified term. Mom made darn sure our money was working for us before we were even old enough to have jobs. And she also made sure no one could access that money for several years, allowing it to grow while we mostly forgot about it.

That money ultimately paid for my first vehicle and part of my university tuition. I still had to take out student loans, but my mom's efforts getting me to save money from childhood helped set me up for the financial stability I obtained in my mid-adult years.

When I returned to Canada after working in Japan, my mom nagged me to open an RRSP account. I mostly did so to get her to stop harping at me about it, but starting with $25 a month when I was twenty-five allowed me to see that money grow over the years. The funds have grown not just because I continue to add to them, but because the investments increase in value and I have learned to manage them to make them grow even more. My RRSP investment then allowed me to put down a decent down payment on my first home and avoid having to pay CMHC fees, and the ripple effect continued from there.

I was lucky that my mom set out to get me going financially when I was still running around barefoot on the farm and playing with my dog. If you are in your twenties, thirties, or forties and are struggling to find your financial footing, though, it is not too late to start. It's never too late to start. Begin by putting aside some potatoes and watch them grow for a year or two before you start to do much with them.

Conclusion

It's hard when you're starting out, but after ten or twenty years, you will see your savings bucket start to fill and your debt bucket start to empty.

Not every strategy in this book will work for you. You probably hate the idea of some of the strategies I have tried. I didn't enjoy being strict with myself, either, but it was more important to me to sacrifice for a while in order to take the overall financial pressure off of myself sooner rather than later.

Your life is different from mine, and your priorities and needs are different from mine. I don't have kids or a spouse, and so I don't have the expenses for music lessons, sports equipment, additional food and clothing, etc., that parents have. I have the freedom to make my own financial decisions without them impacting children or another adult. But I also have never had a spouse or a roommate to help me pay utility bills and split the rent. I have lived alone almost all of my adult life, which has resulted in paying twice as much for rent and mortgage payments over the years than someone sharing a home would have had to pay. But early on, I decided that my introverted self needed to live alone. That was a priority to me, so I always made sure I could afford do that.

Your priorities will be different from mine, and chances are you won't win a $10,000 jackpot at a Las Vegas slot machine. Or maybe you will—and if you do, believe me, I will cheer loudly for you! But my main message is this: Decide what's important to you and focus on that. If nothing in this book appeals to you and you decide to continue living the way you have been, at the very least I hope you have enjoyed my stories. If I have given you some ideas to try, and they work for you, stick with them.

I'm at the point where I subconsciously buy toilet paper every now and then when I see it's on sale and just throw it into the garage. I don't think about a lot of these steps and strategies anymore. After years of playing the games of seeking out sales and looking for discounts, almost all of this is habitual now. If I notice that I could use a new T-shirt, I make a mental note to head to a store on the weekend when shirts will be on sale. When I log into my bank accounts online to pay bills, I check my investments. If they are up a fair bit, I make an appointment to see my investment adviser. We skim profits and rearrange some money so that I'm seeding new growth. This has all become part of my way of life.

Don't be afraid of your money. You work hard for it so that it can bring you pleasure. Find the fun side of managing your money. Make your money work as hard for you as you work for it.

Conclusion

TIP:

Decide on what's most important to you and focus on that.

Glossary

avalanche method The avalanche method means you focus on paying off your loan with the highest interest rate first—and you make minimum payments on all of your other loans. This approach will ultimately save you a great deal of money in interest charges.

banks Unlike credit unions, banks are for-profit, meaning they aim to make money. They offer a wide range of services and products such as chequing, savings, and investment accounts. Banks employ investment advisers, mortgage specialists, and other staff who can help you with your financial needs, from simply depositing and withdrawing money for day-to-day expenses to investing and borrowing money for personal or business use.

capital gains Capital gains can get complicated and confusing. In general, a capital gain is the profit you make on selling an investment—such as real estate, stocks, and other investments—and you will need to pay tax on that profit since it is considered income. Capital gains entail much more than that, but for our purposes, I simply want to let you know that you have to pay income tax on any money that you make on investments, unless the investment is tax-sheltered. Tax-sheltered investments include RRSPs, TFSAs, and RESPs. If you get to the point where your investments are making money, enlist a good accountant to help you calculate how much of an impact the profits have on your income tax.

CMHC: Canada Mortgage and Housing Corporation The CMHC is the government body that regulates the purchase and sale of homes in Canada. You need to follow certain rules and guidelines when purchasing a home, and the CMHC establishes these regulations. For example, you must have at least 5% of the purchase price of the home to put toward the down payment. Also, if your mortgage is 80% or more of the purchase price of your home (i.e., your down payment is less than 20% of the purchase price), you are required to buy CMHC insurance on the loan. The amount of your insurance premiums depends on the amount of your loan (mortgage).

compound earnings The term compound earnings refers to what you earn on the money you have made on an initial investment and then reinvested. Let's say you have an investment account that has earned $10,000. By reinvesting those earnings into a new investment account, the $10,000 then starts to earn returns, as well. These returns are compound earnings. This is one of the best ways to earn: taking money you make from investments and using it to make more money in return.

compound interest Compound interest works the same way as compound earnings except that it's applied to interest. In other words, you pay interest on interest! If your interest charges are racking up on a loan, you will end up being charged interest on the interest you have previously accrued! Paying compound interest means you are going backwards. Compound earnings are great, but paying compound interest quickly siphons money away from you.

CPP: Canada Pension Plan All Canadian workers need to pay into this government program. Contributions are deducted by your employer from your paycheque. The CPP is set up so that Canadians, once they retire or reach age sixty-five, can collect a pension from the government. There have been discussions for years that the CPP is running out of money and will not be there for younger people once they retire, but this has not yet happened. You can monitor your CPP status in your Service Canada account to see how much money you will be eligible to receive upon turning sixty-five. You currently have the option receiving CPP payments starting at age sixty, but these payments will be lower than if you wait until sixty-five.

credit score/credit rating Your credit score, also called a credit rating, is a number that indicates to lenders how much of a risk you are in regard to borrowing and paying back money. Any time you request a loan from a bank or a vehicle dealership, and any time you apply for a credit card or another type of credit, the potential lender will review your credit score. Your credit score is based on a number of factors, including:

- your net worth
- how much debt you have
- how *many* loans you have
- how good you are at paying your bills or making debt payments (any late or missed payments, even on your cellphone bill, will negatively impact your credit score)
- how quickly you have repaid previous loans

The higher your credit score, the better. A score of 800 or higher is considered excellent.

credit union A credit union is similar to a bank. The main differences are that credit unions are not-for-profit, and they are usually smaller and more localized. A credit union offers many of the same services as a bank but *may* have lower fees and higher rates of return.

EI: employment insurance All Canadian workers need to pay into this government program. Your employer deducts the contributions from your paycheque. Canadians who have paid into EI can use it if they lose their job through no fault of their own or are off work for medical reasons. Examples include sick leave, maternity or paternity leave, and caregiver leave.

flipping Flipping is an investment strategy that some people use if they like dealing with real estate. Flipping real estate means buying property, making improvements and renovations, and then selling it for a profit. As with any investment, the goal is to "buy low, sell high." Making money by flipping properties requires a great deal of knowledge and work. Therefore, it is not an easy way to make a dollar if you don't know much about property, the real estate markets, home renovations, etc. Also, keep in mind that any money made on selling the property is subject to tax as capital gains.

FOMO: fear of missing out The idea behind FOMO is that people grab hold of an idea, take part in an activity, make a purchase, etc., that they otherwise wouldn't, but "everyone else is doing it" and they don't want to miss out. Peer pressure, wanting to keep up with the newest trends, and the desire to not miss out pushes people to such activities. FOMO can be a good motivator, but it can also increase anxiety and cause people to overextend themselves physically, mentally, and financially in order to keep up with those around them. For example, feeling left out because friends or neighbours are taking exotic vacations every year may prompt someone to spend money on vacations that then leave them feeling cash-strapped.

HBP: Home Buyers' Plan Canada's Home Buyers' Plan allows first-time homebuyers to withdraw (borrow) up to $35,000 from their RRSP to use for the down payment of a home. You may borrow up to this amount, but you must pay back the borrowed money within fifteen years in order to avoid being taxed.

HELOC: home equity line of credit A home equity line of credit is a type of loan that involves borrowing money and opening a line of credit using the equity in your home as collateral. It operates like a personal line of credit, but in the event that you default on payments to the money owed, your home ownership may be in jeopardy (see *lien* below).

house poor Being house poor means you spend so much of your money on your mortgage, taxes, utilities, furnishings, landscaping, maintenance, etc., that you are strained financially when it comes to paying other bills and saving any money.

lien If your vehicle or home has a lien on it, that means that creditors (people you owe money to) could seize the vehicle or other property if you default on your loan payments. When you are borrowing money for any purpose, lenders will want to know that you are capable of paying them back. Naturally, they will want to see proof that you have money or something of value that they can seize if you fail to pay them back.

mortgage A mortgage is the amount of money that someone borrows to buy a home, whether the property is the borrower's prime residence or an investment property. A mortgage is separate from other debts and loans, and it must be paid off in an agreed-upon time frame. As with any other loan, a minimum payment must be made each month or every two weeks.

passive income Passive income refers to money that you make without having to put time into making it. Passive income can come from real estate or other investments, affiliate links on your blog, or other sources. You set yourself up to earn money off of something that then requires little or no attention from you as it generates income for you.

personal line of credit You can borrow against a personal line of credit for any purpose. Much like a credit card, you can only borrow a limited amount of money and you must pay it back at the set interest rate. Also like a credit card, you must make minimum payments on the balance owing each month. However, personal lines of credit tend to have *much* lower rates of interest than credit cards.

RESP: Registered Education Savings Plan

An RESP is a savings plan you can use to set aside funds for the future post-secondary education of a child (yours or someone else's). You are restricted in how much you can put into the savings plan and what you eventually need to do with the funds. The Canadian government will also add a small amount to the savings in this plan through the Canada Education Savings Grant program.

RRSP: Registered Retirement Savings Plan

An RRSP is a registered savings plan you may contribute to in order to save for retirement. You may contribute a certain percentage of your income each year. Check your income tax assessment from the CRA for your contribution limit. Your contributions are tax-sheltered, meaning your earnings are not taxable. You pay income tax on this money only when you withdraw it, and while you may withdraw money from your RRSP at any time, you are not required to do so until age seventy-one.

snowball method The snowball method of debt payment means that you focus on paying off the debt with the lowest balance first. For any other debts, you'll make the minimum payments. Once the smallest debt has been eliminated, focus on the next smallest, and so on.

tax-sheltered Tax-sheltered investments are those which earn you money without you having to pay much or even any taxes on the earnings. In Canada, TFSA and RRSP accounts are the two of the most common tax-sheltered investments that average people take advantage of.

TFSA: Tax-Free Savings Account A TFSA is an investment account you can use to save money for emergencies or future large purchases such as a vehicle or a down payment for a new home. The earnings on your savings will not be taxed. Despite the name, the account does not have to be a savings account; you can choose from many of the same mutual funds and investment accounts that are also eligible for RRSP investments.

About the Author

Lorna Stuber has a Bachelor of Education degree with a double major in English Language Arts and Social Studies Education (University of Lethbridge), a Diploma in Education specializing in ESL Curriculum and Instruction (University of Calgary), and an Editing Certificate (Simon Fraser University). She spent her twenties teaching ESL in Fujisawa, Japan and Calgary, Canada; and her thirties and forties teaching online high school English, Social Studies, Foods and Nutrition, and Aboriginal Studies courses for the Calgary Board of Education. After resigning from her teaching position, she began freelance editing, writing, and ghostwriting.

Lorna spends most of her money on plane tickets and accommodation in cool and often obscure travel destinations. When she is not helping others fine-tune their writing, she is snowshoeing, volunteering for local theatre, working on her own writing, and fulfilling her duties as a self-appointed "bad-influence auntie" to her friends' kids. She is the owner of Lorna Stuber—Editor, Proofreader, Writer.

Lorna currently lives in Okotoks, Canada, with her dust elephants and her kitchen view of the Rocky Mountains.

Website: lornastuber.com

Facebook: facebook.com/lornastubereditor

LinkedIn: linkedin.com/in/lorna-stuber-freelance-editor-writer-ghostwriter/

Index

A

accountants, 112, 161–164, 208. *see also* income tax; tax returns

accounts
    chequing, 24, 26, 41, 96, 100, 101, 207
    general, 11, 13, 24, 27–29, 35–36, 39, 58, 66
    investments, 30, 207, 215
    RESPs, 7, 25, 90–92, 98, 163, 208, 214
    RRSPs, 24, 35–38, 72–82, 84–85, 87–91, 95–100, 108, 161–162, 194, 199, 202, 208, 212, 214–215
    savings, 3, 24, 26, 74, 83, 96, 207, 215
    TFSAs, 24, 87, 89, 92, 96, 199, 208, 215

advisers
    general, 29, 92–93, 95, 99
    investments, 22, 25, 31, 73, 75–76, 194, 204, 207
    loans, 22

Air Miles, 133, 172. *see also* freebies; perks; reward points; rewards programs

American Express, 64–65. *see also* credit cards; Mastercard; Visa
automatic contributions, 36
automatic deposits, 35
avalanche method, 48–49, 207. *see also* debt reduction; snowball method

B

bad debts, 45–46, 49, 57, 78
bank (client) cards, 38–39, 42, 195
bank accounts. *see* accounts
banks, 6, 21–23, 25–27, 29–31, 37, 52–53, 56, 76, 88, 92, 108, 201, 207
bills, 4, 9–10, 51–52, 204, 210
bonuses, 61, 170
budgets, 39, 59, 65, 67, 105, 143
buy-and-sell groups, 144
buy-nothing groups, 144

C

Canada Mortgage and Housing Corporation. *see* CMHC
Canada Pension Plan. *see* CPP
Canada Revenue Agency. *see* CRA
Canada Savings Bonds, 98, 201
capital gains, 112, 208, 212
cash, 4, 9, 38–42, 59, 63, 90, 106, 108, 133, 174, 186, 193–194
cash flow, 39
charitable donations, 131, 165–167, 176
child care, 163

children, 7, 163, 203
clothing, 7, 10, 17, 33, 58, 106, 148, 171, 199, 203
CMHC, 83, 85, 107, 108, 202, 208
compound earnings, 72, 99, 209
compound interest, 72, 209
consignment stores, 145
contribution limits
    general, 88–89
    RRSPs, 80–81
    TFSAs, 90
contributions
    automatic, 36
    general, 88, 90–91, 214
    RRSPs, 78, 81, 87, 88, 162
    TFSAs, 88–89
Costco memberships, 132, 156
COVID-19, 4, 39, 43, 67, 69, 136, 197, 198. *see also* pandemics
CPP, 35, 37, 72, 209, 210
CRA, 78, 82, 163, 194, 214
credit, 34, 45, 54, 64, 133
credit cards
    American Express, 64–65
    balances, 26, 45–46, 48–49, 52, 54–56, 65, 78, 184
    business, 24–25
    debts, 45, 51
    department stores, 51, 64–65
    general, 4, 6, 23–27, 41–42, 46, 48–55, 61–63, 65–68, 100, 138, 171–172, 210, 214
    interest, 49–50, 55, 64
    limits, 24, 56, 64
    Mastercard, 51, 62, 64–65

Visa, 51, 62, 64–66
Westjet, 26–27, 62
credit limits, 30
credit ratings, 54, 62, 210
credit scores, 54–55, 61, 65, 210–211
credit unions, 22–23, 25, 207, 211

D

deals, 141, 143, 148, 150, 152, 155, 172–173. *see also* discounts; freebies; perks; reward points; rewards programs
debit cards, 38–39, 42, 195
debt management, 67
debt reduction, 6, 14, 33–34, 49, 51, 56–58, 215. *see also* avalanche method; snowball method
debt-to-income-ratio, 3
debts
    credit cards, 45, 51 (*see also* American Express; Mastercard; Visa)
    general, 1, 6, 10, 14, 16, 24, 34, 46, 48, 54, 56, 61–62, 66–67, 78, 106, 203, 210, 213
    levels, 3
deductions. *see* tax deductions
department stores, 61
deposits
    automatic, 35
    general, 11, 37, 87, 100, 189, 194, 207
depreciation, 46
discounts, 148, 151–152, 154–155, 157, 171, 204. *see also* deals; freebies; perks; promotions; reward points; rewards programs

dollar stores, 144
donations, 131, 165–167, 176
down payments, 82, 84, 107–108, 208, 212

E

earnings, 72, 99–100, 209, 215. *see also* income; profits; tax-sheltered income
EI, 37, 211
emergencies, 5, 24, 34, 74, 89, 101
Employment Insurance. *see* EI
equity, 85
exemptions, 163
expenses
    business, 116
    children, 163
    general, 4, 7, 40, 103, 106–107, 110, 116, 163–164, 207
    health, 164
    house, 30, 85

F

Facebook, 1, 136, 139, 144, 158, 175, 187
Facebook Marketplace, 144, 158, 177
fear of missing out. *see* FOMO
fees
    banks, 100–101
    CMHC, 83, 85
    credit cards, 101
    general, 17, 23, 27, 63, 101, 159, 211
    insurance, 108
    schools, 7

financial advisers, 21–22, 29–31, 49, 73, 75–76, 92–93, 99, 194, 204, 207
financial freedom, 2–3, 6, 14–16
financial goals, 14–15
financial hardships, 3
financial management, 1
financial needs, 23
financial rewards, 6
financial stablility, 3, 6, 85, 109, 202
financial stress, 4, 6, 12, 14–16, 18, 22, 41, 49–50, 103. *see also* mentality; psychological rewards
Flashfood, 156
FOMO, 138, 141, 212
freebies, 137–138, 171, 174–175. *see also* deals; perks; reward points; rewards programs
furnishings, 84, 145, 213

G

garage sales, 9, 140, 144–145, 176. *see also* rummage sales
gift cards, 170
good debts, 45, 66, 78
groceries, 10–11, 14, 17, 57, 66, 68, 106, 119, 133, 148, 153–154, 157
grocery stores, 120, 132–133, 149–151, 154, 156, 171–172

H

HBP, 82–83, 85, 89, 108, 212
HELOC, 31, 212
Home Buyer's Plan. *see* HBP

home equity lines of credit. *see* HELOC
home ownership, 82–83, 85, 108, 148
home renovations, 85, 89, 111–112, 156, 171, 211
home repairs, 111
homebuyers, 108, 212
homeowner expenses, 85
household appliances, 84, 145, 176. *see also* kitchen appliances
housing, 10, 17, 45, 54, 58, 84, 139, 208, 213, 215

I

income, 35, 84, 92, 100, 103, 112, 175, 183, 192, 214. *see also* earnings; net income; profits; tax-sheltered income
income tax
    deductions, 35, 37–38, 77, 100, 106–107, 116, 131, 166–167
    general, 35, 72, 77, 79, 83, 88, 159, 162, 194, 208, 215
interest
    compound, 72, 109
    credit cards, 50
    general, 17, 34, 46, 48–57, 59, 64–65, 68, 78–81, 91, 98, 104–105, 113, 209
    lines of credit, 56
    rates, 23, 26–29, 53, 55–56, 64, 207, 214
investments
    accounts, 24–25, 27–30, 35–36, 39, 45–46, 58, 66, 88–89, 96–97, 162, 207, 215
    advisers, 21–22, 29–31, 49, 73, 75–76, 92–93, 95, 99, 194, 204, 207
    companies, 76, 88, 92
    education, 45, 66

    general, 28–31, 38, 71, 75–77, 92, 97–101, 109–110, 113, 124, 201–202, 204, 208–209, 211, 214
    goals, 29, 96
    real estate, 7, 45, 108, 112, 208, 213
    RESPs, 7, 25, 73, 90–92, 98, 163, 208, 214
    returns, 77, 92, 99, 112, 197, 199
    RRSPs, 37, 72–75, 88, 95, 100, 162, 202, 208, 215
    tax-sheltered, 72, 88, 162, 208, 215
    TFSAs, 73, 87–90, 92, 96, 199, 205, 208
IRS, 194

K

kids, 7, 163, 203
Kijiji, 175
kitchen appliances, 10. *see also* household appliances

L

landlords, 109–110
lenders, 54, 106
lending rates, 55. *see also* interest, rates
liens, 113, 213
lines of credit
    general, 30–31, 46, 51, 55, 65–66, 80, 212
    home equity, 31, 212
    interest, 56
    personal, 24–25, 30, 48, 213, 214
    RRSP, 78, 80

loans
    advisers, 22
    general, 12, 16, 46, 49–51, 54, 57–58, 65, 79, 80, 207, 210, 212
    high interest, 55
    mortgages, 45–46, 50, 58
    payments, 12–14
    repayment, 82
    students, 2, 11–12, 28, 45, 48, 51, 56, 58, 66, 140, 202
    terms, 59
    vehicles, 45, 46–48, 51, 56, 58
loyalty programs
    Air Miles, 133, 172
    credit cards, 52
    general, 27, 171

M

Mastercard, 51, 62, 64–65. *see also* American Express; credit cards; Visa
membership discounts, 155. *see also* Costco memberships; loyalty programs; reward points; rewards programs
mentality, 7, 9, 15, 18, 101, 135. *see also* financial stress; psychological rewards
money management, 9, 37, 62
mortgages
    brokers, 106
    general, 21, 25, 29, 45–46, 50–51, 58–59, 78, 85, 103–109, 112–113, 180, 184, 203, 208, 213
    specialists, 207
    terms, 58–59, 104–105, 113
mutual funds, 28, 88

N

negotiations, 56, 148
net income, 36, 38, 106. *see also* income

O

online banking, 196
overspending, 37, 136

P

pandemics, 4–5, 42, 68, 198, 199. *see also* COVID-19
passive income, 177–181, 213
paycheques, 3, 35–38, 41, 77, 79, 105, 159, 209, 211
payments
    credit cards, 50
    frequency, 59, 62
    general, 47, 50, 57, 62, 112, 113
    interest, 104
    loans, 213
    lump-sums, 59, 113
    minimums, 59, 62, 106, 112, 207, 214–215
    mortgages, 50, 59, 103–107, 113, 203
    vehicles, 47, 51, 90, 120
penalties, 56, 159
pension
    accounts, 38
    contributions, 36
    general, 36, 184, 209
    plans, 37, 72–73

perks, 21, 26–27, 53, 62–64, 170, 173. *see also* deals; discounts; freebies; reward points; rewards programs; sales
principal, 59, 105, 107, 112–113
priorities, 16, 48, 58, 203, 204
profits, 30–31, 97–99, 112, 197, 199, 204, 208. *see also* earnings; tax-sheltered income
promotions, 21, 150–151, 154–155
properties, 111, 211
property management, 110
psychological rewards, 6, 41, 49. *see also* financial stress; mentality
purchases
   general, 67, 108
   homes, 7 (*see also* home ownership; real estate)

R

real estate, 108, 112, 208, 211, 213
Registered Education Savings Plans. *see* RESPs
Registered Retirement Savings Plans. *see* RRSPs
reinvesting, 99. *see also* compound earnings
renovations. *see* home renovations
rent, 85, 103, 109–110, 203
rental properties, 108. *see also* landlords; renters
renters, 109–110. *see also* landlords; rental properties
RESPs, 7, 25, 73, 90–92, 98, 163, 208, 214
retirement
   general, 2, 5, 38, 71–72, 76, 103, 184, 210
   plans, 36
   savings, 34, 36 (*see also* RRSPs)
returns, 28, 189, 198–199, 209
reward points, 26–27, 42, 63, 65, 68, 132–133, 156, 170–172

rewards
    financial, 6
    general, 21, 26
    psychological, 6, 41, 49 (*see also* mentality)
rewards programs
    Air Miles, 133, 172
    credit card, 52
    general, 27, 171
risk tolerance, 25, 75, 92, 96, 109, 112, 195
RRSPs
    contribution deadlines, 79
    general, 35–38, 72–80, 82, 84–85, 87–88, 91, 95–97, 100,
            108, 161, 194, 199, 202, 208, 212, 214–215
rummage sales, 145–147. *see also* garage sales

S

salaries, 5, 112
sales, 133, 143, 148, 150, 152–154, 156, 204. *see also* deals;
        discounts; freebies; perks
savings
    Canada Savings Bonds, 98, 201
    emergency, 5, 11
    general, 33–38, 40–42, 73, 82–83, 87, 89–90, 96, 98, 105–
            107, 113, 147–148, 156, 196, 203
    retirement, 34, 36, 71, 73 (*see also* RRSPs)
scholarships, 184–185
Service Canada, 210
snowball method, 48–49, 51, 215. *see also* avalanche method;
        debt reduction

Index

stores
    consignment, 145
    department, 61
    dollar, 144
    groceries, 120, 132–133, 149–151, 154, 156, 171–172
    thrift, 144–145, 157, 175–176
strategies, 1, 6–7, 16, 29, 40, 98, 122–123, 203–204, 211
stress, financial, 4, 7–10
student loans, 2, 11–12, 28, 45, 48, 51, 56, 58, 66, 140, 202

T

take-home pay. *see* net income
tax assessments, 78, 81, 214
tax brackets, 112
tax deductions
    general, 35, 37–38, 77, 84, 100, 116, 131, 160–164, 166–167
    tuition, 161
tax documents, 193
Tax Free Savings Plan. *see* accounts, TFSAs; TFSAs
tax implications, 112
tax payable, 90–92, 208
tax receipts, 165
tax refunds, 77, 79–80, 87, 91, 160–162
tax returns, 79–81, 159–161, 163. *see also* accountants; TurboTax
tax-sheltered income, 81–82, 88–90, 162, 208, 214–215. *see also* earnings; profits
taxable income, 192. *see also* income; net income
taxes, 74, 212–213, 215. *see also* income tax
TFSAs, 73, 87–90, 92, 96, 199, 208, 215
thrift stores, 144–145, 157, 175–176

transportation, 10
travel, 10, 62, 67–69, 84, 172–174, 188. *see also* vacations
tuition, 45, 84, 91, 161, 185, 201–202
TurboTax, 160. *see also* tax returns

V

vacations, 10, 33–34, 41–42, 48, 50, 58, 67, 69, 89, 101, 113, 139, 174, 186–188, 198–199, 212. *see also* travel
VarageSale, 144, 175
vehicles
    general, 10, 33, 46–47, 54, 58, 84, 89–90, 93, 98, 120, 130, 134, 139–140, 148, 151, 155, 171, 184, 202, 215
    loans, 45–47, 56, 210, 213
    payments, 106
    repairs, 118
    upgrades, 41
Visa, 51, 62, 64–66. *see also* American Express; credit cards; Mastercard

W

Westjet (credit cards), 26–27, 62
withdrawal limits, 85
withdrawals, 87–89, 91, 100, 207, 215

Bibliography & Additional Reading

Barker, Eric. "This Is the Best Way to Overcome Fear of Missing Out." Time. June 7, 2016.
https://time.com/4358140/overcome-fomo.

Barone, Adam. "Bank." Investopedia. Updated March 21, 2021.
https://www.investopedia.com/terms/b/bank.asp.

Brown, Jordann. "Banks vs. Credit Unions in Canada: What's the Difference?" Ratehub.ca. March 9, 2020.
https://www.ratehub.ca/blog/banks-vs-credit-unions-in-canada.

Caldwell, Miriam. "Mortgage Questions: Are You House Poor?" The Balance. Updated July 2, 2021.
https://www.thebalance.com/are-you-house-poor-2385832.

Cambridge Dictionary, s. v., "keep up with the Joneses" accessed October 26, 2020, https://dictionary.cambridge.org/dictionary/english/keep-up-with-the-joneses.

Chen, James. "Compounding." Investopedia. Updated February 23, 2021.
https://www.investopedia.com/terms/c/compounding.asp.

Clark, Biron. "What to Do With Extra Money Each Month: 10 Ideas." Career Sidekick. Accessed September 14, 2021.
https://careersidekick.com/what-to-do-with-extra-money.

creditcardGenius Team. "How Credit Card Interest Works in Canada." creditcardGenius. Updated May 3, 2021.
https://creditcardgenius.ca/blog/how-credit-card-interest-works-in-canada.

Credit Counselling Society. "Consumer Debt Report 2020." Accessed September 15, 2021.
https://nomoredebts.org/consumer-debt-report-2020.

Eneriz, Ashley. "Debt Avalanche vs. Debt Snowball: What's the Difference?" April 28, 2021.
https://www.investopedia.com/articles/personal-finance/080716/debt-avalanche-vs-debt-snowball-which-best-you.asp.

Fernando, Jason. "Compound Interest." Investopedia. Updated February 16, 2021.
https://www.investopedia.com/terms/c/compoundinterest.asp.

Goldman, Andrew. "Emergency Funds: What, Why & How Much." Wealthsimple. Updated March 15, 2021.
https://www.wealthsimple.com/en-ca/learn/emergency-funds.

Government of Canada. "Apply for the Canada Education Savings Grant (CESG) — About the Grant." Modified May 3, 2019. https://www.canada.ca/en/services/benefits/education/education-savings/savings-grant.html.

—. "Capital Gains — 2020." Modified January 18, 2021. https://www.canada.ca/en/revenue-agency/services/forms-publications/publications/t4037/capital-gains.html.

—. "CPP Retirement Pension: Overview." Modified August 12, 2021. https://www.canada.ca/en/services/benefits/publicpensions/cpp.html.

—. "Employment Insurance Benefits and Leave." Modified August 31, 2021. https://www.canada.ca/en/services/benefits/ei.html.

—. "Family, Child Care, and Caregivers Deductions and Credits." Modified January 18, 2021. https://www.canada.ca/en/revenue-agency/services/tax/individuals/topics/about-your-tax-return/tax-return/completing-a-tax-return/deductions-credits-expenses/family-child-care-caregivers-deductions-credits.html.

—. "Lines of Credit." Modified March 21, 2019. https://www.canada.ca/en/financial-consumer-agency/services/loans/loans-lines-credit.html.

—. "Money and Finances." Modified July 14, 2021. https://www.canada.ca/en/services/finance.html.

—. "Registered Education Savings Plans." Modified May 3, 2019. https://www.canada.ca/en/services/benefits/education/education-savings/resp.html.

—. "Registered Retirement Savings Plan (RRSP)." Modified January 7, 2021. https://www.canada.ca/en/revenue-agency/services/tax/individuals/topics/rrsps-related-plans/registered-retirement-savings-plan-rrsp.html.

—. "Service Canada." Modified August 31, 2021. https://www.canada.ca/en/employment-social-development/corporate/portfolio/service-canada.html.

—. "Tax-Free Savings Account (TFSA), Guide for Individuals." Modified January 25, 2021. https://www.canada.ca/en/revenue-agency/services/forms-publications/publications/rc4466/tax-free-savings-account-tfsa-guide-individuals.html.

—. "What is the Home Buyers' Plan (HBP)?" Modified December 9, 2019. https://www.canada.ca/en/revenue-agency/services/tax/individuals/topics/rrsps-related-plans/what-home-buyers-plan.html.

Grant, Mitchell. "Credit Union." Investopedia. Updated February 24, 2021. https://www.investopedia.com/terms/c/creditunion.asp.

Hardekopf, Bill. "Do People Really Spend More with Credit Cards?" Forbes. July 16, 2018. https://www.forbes.com/sites/billhardekopf/2018/07/16/do-people-really-spend-more-with-credit-cards.

Great West Media: Infinite Chartered Professional Accountants & Wealth Planning. "Basic Financial Terms Everyone Should Know." *Okotoks Today*. February 5, 2021. https://www.okotokstoday.ca/finances-fyi/basic-financial-terms-everyone-should-know.

Kagan, Julia. "Debt Snowball." Investopedia. May 8, 2021. https://www.investopedia.com/terms/s/snowball.asp.

—. "What is a Mortgage?" Investopedia. Updated September 8, 2021. https://www.investopedia.com/terms/m/mortgage.asp.

Kalogeropoulos, Demitrios. "Why Royal Caribbean Stock Dove 60% in March." Nasdaq. April 2, 2020. https://www.nasdaq.com/articles/why-royal-caribbean-stock-dove-60-in-march-2020-04-02.

Kenton, Will. "Lien," Investopedia, reviewed April 16, 2021, https://www.investopedia.com/terms/l/lien.asp.

Kurt, Daniel. "A Guide for Home Equity Loans and HELOCs," Investopedia. Updated September 11, 2021. https://www.investopedia.com/mortgage/heloc.

Labbé, Stefan. "Work from Home? Here's How Canadians Can Get a $400 Tax Deduction." *Okotoks Today*. December 5, 2020. https://www.okotokstoday.ca/beyond-local/work-from-home-heres-how-canadians-can-get-a-400-tax-deduction-3152096.

Lovett-Reid, Patricia. "Pattie Lovett-Reid: Tips from Experts to Take Control of Your Finances." CTV News. January 22, 2021. https://www.ctvnews.ca/business/pattie-lovett-reid-tips-from-experts-to-take-control-of-your-finances-1.5274699.

MacQueen, Alexandra. "Canada's Climbing Debt-to-Income Ratio: What You Need to Know." CIBC Pace It. December 2020. https://www.moneysense.ca/save/debt/canadas-climbing-debt-to-income-ratio-what-you-need-to-know/.

McWhinney, James. "5 Mistakes that Can Make House Flipping a Flop." Investopedia. Updated May 16, 2021. https://www.investopedia.com/articles/mortgages-real-estate/08/house-flip.asp.

MNP Ltd. "Over Half (53%) of Canadians within $200 of Not Being Able to Cover Their Bills and Debt Payments, Up 10 Points Since December Reaching a Five-Year High." April 8, 2021. https://www.globenewswire.com/news-release/2021/04/08/2206577/0/en/Over-Half-53-of-Canadians-Within-200-of-Not-Being-Able-to-Cover-Their-Bills-and-Debt-Payments-Up-10-Points-Since-December-Reaching-a-Five-Year-High.html.

Ratehub.ca. "Mortgage Default Insurance (CMHC Insurance)". Updated January 11, 2021. https://www.ratehub.ca/cmhc-mortgage-insurance.

Ratehub.ca. "Store Credit Cards." Accessed August 23, 2021 from https://www.ratehub.ca/credit-cards/store-credit-cards.

Satov, Tamar. "All You Need to Know About a Line of Credit." GreedyRates. Updated August 7, 2021. https://www.greedyrates.ca/blog/what-is-a-line-of-credit.

Scott, Elizabeth. "How to Deal with FOMO in Your Life." Verywell Mind. Updated April 25, 2021. https://www.verywellmind.com/how-to-cope-with-fomo-4174664.

Spurlock, Morgan, dir. *Super Size Me*. 2004; Appleton, WI, United States: Roadside Attractions.

The Investopedia Team. "Credit Score." Investopedia." Updated March 11, 2021. https://www.investopedia.com/terms/c/credit_score.asp.

Tschir, Jason. "Do Spoilers Actually Improve a Car's Performance?" *The Globe and Mail*. October 21, 2014. https://www.theglobeandmail.com/globe-drive/culture/commuting/do-spoilers-actually-improve-a-cars-performance/article21180268.

Waits, Kentin. "7 Ways Psychologists Say Saving Boosts Your Mental Health." WiseBread. December 15, 2014. https://www.wisebread.com/7-ways-psychologists-say-saving-boosts-your-mental-health.

www.ingramcontent.com/pod-product-compliance
Lightning Source LLC
Chambersburg PA
CBHW020903080526
44589CB00011B/427